Landscape with Weapon

Joe Penhall lives in London. *Some Voices* (Royal Court Theatre Upstairs, 1994) won him a Thames Television Bursary and the John Whiting Award in 1995. *Pale Horse* (Royal Court Theatre Upstairs, 1995) won the Thames Television Best Play Award. *Love and Understanding* (Bush Theatre, 1997) and *The Bullet* (Donmar Warehouse, 1998) preceded *Blue/Orange* (Cottesloe Theatre, National Theatre, 2000), which won the *Evening Standard* Best Play Award, the Olivier Award for Best New Play 2001 and the Critics' Circle Award for Best New Play 2000. His most recent work for the stage was *Dumb Show* (Royal Court Theatre Jerwood Theatre Downstairs, 2004). His film and television work includes the screenplay *Enduring Love* produced for FilmFour in 2004, and *The Long Firm*, a four-part serial for the BBC in 2004.

T0258346

Joe Penhall

Landscape with Weapon

Methuen Drama

Published by Methuen Drama 2007

1 3 5 7 9 10 8 6 4 2

Methuen Drama
A & C Black Publishers Limited
38 Soho Square
London W1D 3HB
www.acblack.com

ISBN: 978 0 713 68805 4

A CIP catalogue record for this book is available from the British Library

Typeset by Country Setting, Kingsdown, Kent
Printed and bound in Great Britain by
Bookmarque Ltd, Croydon, Surrey

For the engineers:
Ned Gloster, Simon Brooks and my brother

Landscape with Weapon

Landscape with Weapon was first presented at the Cottesloe Theatre, National Theatre, London, on 29 March 2007. The cast was as follows:

Ned	Tom Hollander
Dan	Julian Rhind-Tutt
Ross	Pippa Haywood
Brooks	Jason Watkins

Director	Roger Michell
Designer	William Dudley
Lighting designer	Rick Fisher
Sound designer	Rich Walsh

Characters

Ned
Dan
Ross
Brooks

The action takes place during summer and autumn in Ned's flat in Earls Court and the aircraft factory where he works, just outside London.

Act One

One

Ned's flat in Earls Court.

Ned is standing in his pyjamas, staring into space, thinking.

The intercom sounds with a buzz.

Silence.

Another buzz.

Frantic buzzing.

Eventually he presses the intercom button.

Dan (*over intercom*)   Ned? Hey, Ned, it's Daniel.

Ned   Hi.

Dan (*over intercom*)   Hi . . . (*Pause.*) Are you going to let me in?
Ned? Neddy?

Ned *releases the downstairs door with a sigh.*

Dan (*over intercom*)   I didn't get it. Ned, I didn't get it.

Ned *releases it again.*

Ned   You get it?

Dan   I didn't get it again.

Ned *releases again.*

Dan   Oh I see, hold on, I got it.

There's the noise of **Dan** *tramping upstairs.*

Ned *goes off to let him in, smoothing his hair.*

Dan (*off*)   Hi.

Ned (*off*)   Hi, Dan.

Dan (*off*)   How you doing?

Ned (*off*)   OK. How are you doing?

Dan (*off*)   Yeah, no, I'm good . . .

Ned comes back in with his brother **Dan***, well dressed, sweating from the heat.*

Dan   Cor it's hot our there. *Scorchio.* Don't you just love global warming? I'm serious, I really like it . . .

He eyes **Ned** *up and down.*

Dan   I didn't get you up, did I?

Ned   No, I was just . . . you know . . . thinking.

Dan   'Thinking'?

Ned   Yeah, just . . . standing about . . . thinking. Don't you ever do that?

Dan (*thinks*)   No.

Ned   You want a beer?

Dan   It's a bit early. We could start with a cup of coffee and then, you know . . . progress . . .

He looks around.

So this is your new gaff?

Ned   Yeah . . .

Dan   You working from home now?

Ned   Y— sometimes.

Dan   Great location, this is going to be worth a bomb one day.

Ned   I'm just renting.

Dan   Oh, it's not . . . ?

Ned   It's just while I sort things out with Janie.

Dan   A bachelor pad.

Ned   Yes, Dan, 'a bachelor pad'.

Ned *goes to the kitchen. We hear him put beans in an electric grinder and grind them.*

Dan   One day you won't be able to buy a place in this part of town for love nor money. It'll be all gone. All snapped up. In fact, what's happening now is all the mega-rich fuckers are moving in and money's not an object. People are getting gazumped all over the shop. They just go, 'Another fifty grand? Why certainly, sir, I'll fetch my chequebook.'

Ned *(off)*   Cunts.

Dan   We got gazumped twice buying the new place.

Ned *(off)*   Twice?

Dan   In the end we just decided to play the fucking game. I'm mortgaged to the nuts now. But one day . . . I'm playing the long game.

Ned *(off)*   Well, I'm not playing any game, I'm just trying to get set up. *(He returns, screwing together a Bialetti.)* Obviously there's still a chance I could, you know, get back with Janie.

Dan   OK, wow.

Ned   I could use the space if she decides to pop one out.

Dan   It's about time. Inseminate her at once. What's the hold-up?

Ned   We've split up, Dan, that's one obstacle.

He goes off to put the Bialetti on the hob.

Dan   No, but I mean . . . why didn't you ever . . . I mean, before?

Ned *(off)*   Well, you see, I just don't think we were doing it right.

Dan *(beat)*   Uh-huh.

Ned *(off)*   I think I was probably putting it in the wrong hole or something.

Dan *(beat)*   It happens to the best of us.

Ned (*off*)   Plus I like masturbating. I probably wasted all my juice.

Dan   Uh-huh . . . (*Pause.*) Have you seen her lately?

Ned (*returning*)   I see her from time to time. It's it's it's, you know, friendly.

Dan   Well . . . good. Friendly's good.

Ned   Yeah . . . it is, it's nice.

Silence. They eye each other.

It's good to see you. You get a day off?

Dan   I'm on holiday.

Ned   Oh. You're not going away?

Dan   Ah, you know, we just thought, just for a change we'd stay in London this year. You know, we've got the house in Castellina now, which is very nice, but we just thought, fuck it, just for once we should have a holiday in town. You know, like normal people.

Ned   Slum it.

Dan   Yeah . . .

Ned   With the proles.

Dan   Why not?

Ned   With people like me.

Dan   That's the idea.

Ned   This doesn't sound like you. Everything OK?

Dan   Yeah, no, yeah, you know – I've just got a lot of work on.

Ned   How's the practice?

Dan   Fine. I've started this programme which I'm really, you know, passionate about . . . a training thing . . . I'm expanding the practice.

Ned   Training? Really?

Dan   Yeah, it's a new . . . thing.

Ned   Uh-huh. What?

Dan   I don't really wanna talk about it till it happens. In case it, you know, doesn't.

Ned   OK, I understand.

Pause.

Dan   Anyway, I thought we could head out and, you know, you want some lunch? Get some *yum chao*. Line the stomach before we . . . There's a noodle place I quite like opposite the tube. It's not as good as my favourite noodle place in Waterloo, but it's, it's pretty good, pretty good noodles.

Ned   I don't know that place.

Dan   This isn't as good, but it's . . .

Ned   It's OK.

Dan   It's not great but it's . . .

Ned   'Fit for purpose.'

Dan   Mm.

Ned   Actually I've got someone coming round.

Dan   Oho.

Ned   So I really should . . .

Dan   A lady?

Ned   What do you mean?

Dan   Is it a lady?

Ned   She's just coming to talk about something. It is not what you think it is.

Dan   What do I think it is? (*Thinks.*)

Ned (*checking his watch*)   Actually, I should probably –

Dan   OK, no, yeah . . .

Ned   – start getting ready.

Dan   I don't mind, you do what you like . . . I just haven't seen you for a while. You've been away most of the year.

Ned   I know . . . it's been crazy.

Dan   I've hardly spoken to Janie . . . She says she never speaks to you.

Ned   She said that, did she?

Dan   Yeah, what's the story?

Ned   It's a long story . . . I don't really want to get into it now.

Ned *returns to the kitchen.*

Dan   How was California? Did you have a good time? How was the weather? Were you besieged by beautiful but essentially repressed young women going bananas for your cute accent, driving you around in hotted-up cars, offering you their firm, nubile bodies in the back of the 'little deuce coupe' in exchange for, you know, 'the secret plans' and all that? Eh? Eh?

Pause. **Ned** *returns with coffee.*

Ned   How did you know about that?

Dan   Eh?

Ned   How did you know . . . I was in California?

Dan   I knew you were in America. Was it California?

Ned   Where else was I?

Dan   Eh?

Ned   Where else in America was I? On this trip.

Dan   I don't know. All the usual. Nevada. New England?

Ned   Who told you this?

Dan   I don't know. Mum probably.

Ned Mum told you I was in New England?

Dan Probably, yeah, I don't remember.

Ned And Mum told you I was in Nevada? Who else knows?

Dan I don't know. (*Beat.*) Knows what?

Ned Because, you know I'm not supposed to tell anybody this stuff. Not even Janie.

Dan I think you can tell Janie. (*Beat.*) Tell her what?

Ned I could tell her where I was going but to be perfectly honest I couldn't tell her what I was doing.

Dan You couldn't even tell your own wife?

Ned Yeah, I signed a gagging order.

Dan What like a, some corporate . . . ?

Ned Like the Official Secrets Act.

Dan (*beat*) Uh-huh.

Ned I really did. I really can't tell you – rules are rules.

He hands **Dan** *his cup of coffee.*

Dan *blows on his coffee.*

They slurp their coffee.

Silence.

Ned OK . . . It's no big deal . . . I've finished the programme.

Dan Great. Wow . . . (*Beat.*) Which programme?

Ned How many programmes have I been working on?

Dan I know, but I don't know what it is. I don't know how many, you know . . . I don't know anything . . .

Ned Anyway . . . we're doing a deal with the government. They've finally agreed to finance it.

Dan With the government? Wow.

Ned   Yeah, it's good news.

Dan   Cos cos you were pretty uptight about that, weren't you?

Ned   Well, I was –

Dan   Tense. You were tense. On edge. I could tell.

Ned   Well, it was hanging in the balance for so long. It's like anything. I just need to know where I stand.

Dan   I'm exactly the same. I don't like to be jerked about. I like to be my own boss.

Ned   Yeah, well, I think we broke the deadlock. It all sounds pretty positive. They were just being very slow about it.

Dan   Who's they?

Ned   The Ministry of Defence.

Dan (*beat*)   Uh-huh . . .

Ned   We're trying to get them to fund manufacture. The trouble is, their terms are impossible. I mean, basically they'll consider funding development, but not until it's finished.

Dan   I don't get it.

Ned   They won't fund the development until it's developed. Then they'll just buy it. And they'll want a share of the IP.

Dan   What's IP?

Ned   The intellectual property.

Dan   Ah. Never give that up.

Ned   But they haven't contributed anything to development, so why should they share the IP? We didn't even give the Americans a share of the IP. It's insane.

Dan   I don't understand. What Americans?

Ned   Just a private engineering firm, in New England. We contracted them to help finish off a few things.

Dan   Uh-huh . . .

Ned   They gave us the simulator. Better wind tunnel. The strip in Nevada.

Dan   There's nothing like a strip in Nevada.

Ned   A condo. Swimming pool. Tennis court. Tickets to the Hollywood Bowl . . .

Dan   Now we're talking – now we are speaking.

Ned   But we never agreed to share the IP. No way.

Dan   No chance. That's your nest egg. I mean, that's going to pay your house off. You'll be able to buy, you know, a couple of these, a house in the country, get a nice little country pile, maybe buy a house in Castellina . . . You could get a place near me. In fact the guy next door, Franco, OK, his wife's name is Franca, really nice people, he's selling his vineyard . . . you should steam in there.

Ned   Well . . . I intend to.

Dan   That's really amazing. You've hit the jackpot.

Ned   Well, it's early days –

Dan   No, but you know, you get a patent and you own the the the intellectual property and you start selling the fucker to the government . . . you're gonna be *rich*.

Pause.

Ned   Mm . . .

Dan   You are. You're gonna be *rich*.

Ned (*reluctant*)   Well . . . I could . . . if I have it my way.

Dan   Well, there is no other way. Go in hard. Use the programme as as as leverage. If they don't give you what you want, you know, take your fucking ball back. Let's be grown up about this.

Pause.

Ned   Yeah.

Dan   Janie must be thrilled.

Ned   What's it got to do with her? Don't talk about this to Janie.

Dan   I'm just thinking aloud.

Ned   Don't talk about this with anybody . . . it's a serious business.

Dan   Sure, OK, no problem.

Ned   This is classified technology.

Dan   No problem. I understand.

Ned   Well, do you?

Dan   I do absolutely, no problem, no problemo.

Silence.

They drink their coffee.

Dan *fidgets a bit.*

Dan   That's exactly what I'm doing.

Ned   What do you mean?

Dan   This is the thing I'm doing that I wasn't going to tell you about but . . . I'll tell you anyway.

Ned   The training thing?

Dan   I've come up with this process – I'm probably going to get a patent out of it – it's a kind of training procedure that only I know. So I'm hoping to be the first and make a shitload of money. (*Beat.*) I'm gonna be rich too.

Ned   What is it? Come on, spit it out.

Dan   It's Botox. I'm doing Botox now.

Ned (*beat*)   W— you're kidding. That doesn't . . . how can you do that?

Dan   I just woke up one morning and the idea was there, steaming, wedged inside my brain, just downloaded itself in the night. And I just thought, 'Fuck it. Why not?'

Ned   Because . . . you're a dentist.

Dan   Exactly, and I'm sick of it. It's depressing. I'll be able to retire in ten years if this goes well – go and live in Tuscany.

Ned   Are you joking?

Dan   I run courses on Saturdays. One-day comprehensive courses for doctors, other dentists, SRNs and RGNs, explaining the insurance implications, how to store it, how to administer it, and then they get hands-on experience in the afternoon. Only we can't call it 'Botox' because it's not a licensed product. We have to call it 'brow-freezing'.

Ned   'Hands-on experience?' You mean, what, they practise on each other?

Dan   Why not?

Ned   Because . . . (*Thinks.*) It's stupid . . . and . . . it's beneath you.

Dan   No no no – it's all about transferable skills. Something you should learn about. I trained everybody in the surgery to inject the patients if they ask for it, so even when I'm not working, I'm earning. Three hundred and twenty-five pounds for a fifteen-minute session. The beauty of it is you can do it while they're having their teeth polished. I'm probably the first in the country. Nobody else is doing it this way.

Ned   I'm not surprised. What are the side effects?

Dan   Don't look down your nose.

Ned   At least I can look down my nose. What are the side effects?

Dan   Nothing.

Ned   No side effects?

Dan   Nope.

Ned   At all?

Dan   No.

Ned   Nothing?

Pause.

Dan   OK, there's this one thing they call 'droopy eye', but that's extremely rare and completely treatable with eye drops. The Dental Association doesn't like it. Worried about lawsuits. But you just get insurance. You do a bit of training, sit an exam, cough up for the equipment, set aside a little time at the surgery . . . Next thing you're buying your place in the sun, or – in my case – a swimming pool for your place in the sun.

Ned   You bought a swimming pool?

Dan   For the kids . . . so they can, they can learn to swim.

Ned   Why don't I have a swimming pool? I'm the mad genius.

Dan   You could if you put your mind to it. I mean, your average dentist has as much understanding of the muscles and nerve-endings in the face as a cosmetic surgeon . . .

Ned *snorts.*

Dan   I paid my dues, it's time I got something back. Why the hell not?

Ned   Doesn't it say in the Hippocratic oath something about 'poisoning'?

Dan   It's not really poison. It's just, it's complicated . . .

Ned   I thought it was snake venom or something . . .

Dan   It's derived from, from that, yeah . . .

Ned   And you stick it in people's faces and the muscles go numb and they can't move their faces any more.

Dan   That's pretty much, that's part of it, yeah . . .

Ned   Just like having a stroke.

Dan   It's a little more sophisticated than that.

Ned   Yeah, but if you boil it down –

Dan   I don't want to 'boil it down'. You boil it down for me. I can make a lot of money out of making ageing strumpets look beautiful. And I happen to get a big bang out of it. What's the problem?

Ned   It's not your job to making ageing strumpets look beautiful, it's your job to make them look like they have teeth.

Dan   I start with teeth and work outwards.

Pause.

Ned   Do you do it to yourself?

Dan   Who cares if I do?

Ned   So you do?

Dan   Of course I don't.

Ned   You hesitated.

Dan   I don't.

Ned   I bet you do.

Dan   I don't.

Ned   Why not?

Dan   Because it wouldn't be appropriate. Because there are regulations.

Ned   It's regulated? Just like a real medical procedure?

Dan   Not much, but enough. So it's not abused.

Ned   Absolutely, you don't wanna abuse it. (*Beat.*) Let me have a look.

*He takes **Dan**'s chin in his hand, studies his face.*

Ned   You're looking a bit wooden.

Dan   Wooden?

Ned   Sort of pinched.

Dan   I always look like this. You're making me tense.

Ned   It doesn't look right.

Dan (*shrugging him off*)   Get out of it.

Ned   What does Nancy think about it? I haven't seen her lately but I'm guessing she could use a shot. Ever tried it on her?

Dan   You'll be laughing on the other side of your face when you see my new car.

Ned   At least I *can* laugh on the other side of my face. What is it?

Dan   I'll show you later. Take you for a spin.

Ned   I don't want a spin, just tell me what it is.

Dan   It's a Jeep.

Ned   You bought a fucking Jeep?

Dan   I bought a brand spanking new, fully imported American Jeep from America.

Ned   You live in Shepherd's Bush.

Dan   There's a lot of potholes in Shepherd's Bush.

Ned   You penis.

Dan   It's a good safe car for the family.

Ned   Don't use your children to justify it.

Dan   You'd do the same. You think it's wrong?

Ned   I don't know. I just think it's, you know, weird.

Dan   Well, I think what you do is weird . . . disappearing off to America all the time . . . having strange women around . . .

Ned   I think what I do is weird too, but I think what you do is weirder. I mean, at least there's a point to what I do.

Dan   There's a point to what I do. It pays the school fees.

Ned   Well, that's not why I do what I do.

Dan   Why do you do it then?

Ned   Because I believe in it.

Dan (*beat*)   What do you mean?

Ned   I believe in what I do.

Dan   What do you mean?

Ned   I don't just do it for money.

Dan (*blank*)   I don't understand what you mean. Does not compute.

Ned   Don't mock me.

Dan   So what is it? Come on. If you believe in it, if it's so important, such a profoundly important enterprise . . . what exactly is this thing you're selling to the government?

Ned (*beat*)   It's complicated . . . I'll tell you some other time . . .

Dan   No, go on, I'm curious.

Ned   Well. I don't really feel like telling you about it right now.

Dan   Go on, I'm intrigued. I told you about mine.

Ned   Sorry, Dan, I can't tell anybody about this.

Dan   Why not?

Ned   I told you why not.

Dan   But I'm family.

Ned   Makes no difference.

He paces about a bit, considering.

It's just difficult to explain . . .

Dan   Try me.

Ned   It's just a new type of technology. Which I'm developing . . . with the military . . .

Dan   With the *military*?

Ned   Yeah.

Dan   Military technology?

Ned   Yeah, it's military technology.

Dan (*beat*)   What sort of military technology?

Ned   Well, it's . . . like I said, it's classified.

Dan   Just tell me.

Ned   It's just a new kind of . . . system for flying various things . . .

Dan   'Flying various things'? What things?

Ned   Just, you know, unmanned air vehicles . . . UAVs. You know . . . drones.

Dan   'Drones'?

Ned   It's what they've been using in the Middle East. Sometimes we call them 'aerobots'. OK? Flying robots the size of a, of a, of a big bird . . . OK? With tiny cameras for surveillance . . . made out of super-light alloy . . . in completely unorthodox shapes like wedges and discs to help them manoeuvre . . .

Dan   Like flying saucers?

Ned   Yeah, that's what UFOs are in real life. If you go to certain locations in the Nevada Desert the sky is full of them. You'll think you're tripping. People who really are tripping have stumbled upon them and freaked out completely. (*Becoming excited.*) The trouble is, you can't fly them inside buildings because they lose their satellite navigation . . . they lose contact with the global positioning system . . . and if they get shot down, it's incredibly expensive because of all the complex navigational equipment on board. But – using my new technology – once they're out of range of GPS they rely only on each other to navigate.

Dan   How do they do that?

Ned OK, this is the interesting bit: think about the starlings you see on the river, circling over Hammersmith Bridge. Have you seen them?

Pause. **Dan** *thinks.*

Ned You see them forming figures of eight, or vast halos, they form a shape, then as one they all shift and the shape changes. Perfect figures . . . intricate formations . . . Nobody knows why they do it . . . nobody knows what it means . . . all we know is that it's essentially very simple, intuitive emergent behaviour resulting in complex, beautiful, organic movement. Like an invisible magic wand is waved. There's nobody leading them – they position themselves with total precision by communicating with each other. What I've done is found a way to make this work with *aerobots*.

Dan I still don't . . . What's . . . what's the military got to do with it?

Ned I've developed an application for military drones so that in certain situations they won't need to rely on satellite navigation – they'll develop their own emergent behaviour and navigate themselves. You could send them down the tube!

He drinks his coffee.

You sure you don't want a beer?

Dan (*increasingly worried*)   So . . . but, but these . . . drones . . . what do they actually do?

Ned All sorts of things. The point is that as a swarm they can do what they can't do alone. A new behaviour emerges.

Dan Yes, but . . . exactly what are they being used for in the Middle East?

Ned Well, you know, they started out as surveillance vehicles but, you see, what they've done now is weaponised them . . .

Dan 'Weaponised'?

Ned Put weapons on board. In places like Basra or Baghdad or the Gaza Strip – which are basically just nests of concrete

full of rebel militia – it's too dangerous to fly in helicopters.
Unmanned vehicles are the only way to go.

Dan (*slow-dawning anxiety*)   So they're . . . they're not just for
surveillance? They're attack drones?

Ned (*putting coffee down*)   Yeah – they were trying to kill
Saddam Hussein for ages with the fuckers – but he kept going
inside.

Dan (*increasingly bemused*)   Inside where?

Ned   His palace. So then they just basically bombed
everything and they still didn't get him. They couldn't get
Osama bin Laden cos he was in a cave. The big hope for the
future is that, in a *swarm*, they'll descend on a palace – a cave –
a warren of alleyways and –

Dan   You're making me nervous now.

Ned (*enjoying* **Dan**'s *nervousness*)   BAM!

He smacks his fist into his palm violently.

They're in! (*Rapidly, snapping his fingers to punctuate.*) Some are
conducting surveillance – some are finding targets, some are
taking out supply lines – some are repelling enemy fire – a
rebel cell – a nest of safe houses – an entire town – picked
clean – they eat it up like locusts on a stick of corn! It'll make
guided missiles look like nutcrackers . . . it'll be like a symphony
in the sky!

Ned *is animated, pleased with himself.*

Dan *just stands there, staring.*

Dan   Ned . . . this is a pretty frightening concept . . . I mean
to normal people . . . to people who are, you know, not insane.

Ned   Yes! Exactly – because – no, listen – as well as being a
weapon . . . it's a 'deterrent'. A-a-a-a psychological weapon, it's
so frightening and and and appalling . . . it works without even
being used, do you follow what I'm saying?

Dan   No . . .

Ned Nobody wanted nuclear weapons, but like it or not they prevented World War Three. For forty years they prevented a war with Russia. It's ugly but it's true.

Dan Are you . . . are you kidding? This is a joke, surely?

Ned No. Why would I be kidding?

Dan It's insane.

Ned It sounds insane, yes – but –

Dan It's it's its nuts!

Ned No no, it *sounds* nuts –

Dan Because it *is* nuts!

Ned These things always sound nuts in the years before they become a reality. Sixty years ago a computer the size of a paperback sounded nuts. Now it's old hat.

Dan I'm appalled by what you're telling me!

Ned No, it's the future. It's it's it's letting the genie out of the bottle and seeing what it's got for us.

Dan You're making weapons of mass destruction! And and and you're my brother! And and and and I didn't even know!

Pause.

Ned That's not funny.

Dan But that's what it is, isn't it?

Ned It's not 'weapons of mass destruction'.

Dan It sounds like weapons of mass destruction.

Ned Shut up, Dan, OK? Shut up, just shut your fucking cakehole. You don't know what you're talking about. (*Pause.*) You weren't listening properly. For your information – not that it's any of your business – it's entirely different . . . (*Pause.*) You have no idea of the brilliance of the avionics for a start –

Dan A swarm of of of of of of of of of killer-drones?

Ned   You have to remember that primarily it's surveillance equipment, it's just been weaponised, that's all.

Dan   ARE YOU SERIOUS? ARE YOU MAD?!

He staggers a few steps, shocked, head in hands.

Ned   OK, just calm down . . .

Dan   You'll kill . . . loads of people.

Ned   Well, you see, in actual fact I'll kill *less* people.

Dan   What?

Ned   It'll kill *less* people, because it's so accurate.

Dan   Less than what?

Ned   Less than . . . normal. Less than conventional weapons like two-thousand-pound bombs and cluster bombs and nuclear warheads and rockets . . . It eliminates collateral damage . . . it'll eliminate civilian deaths.

Dan   By sending in, what, flying killer-robots?

Ned   You think we should only use people to kill people? You think using robots is *wrong*?

Dan   No, Ned, I think it's *lazy*.

Ned   The Koreans have invented a robot sentry guard. You go up to the gate and if you don't identify yourself properly it blows your head off. They're on the market now. Only trouble is, they can't go down steps.

Dan   Just like Daleks.

Ned   Exactly like Daleks, oddly enough.

Dan (*stares, increasingly freaked out*)   Maybe I will have that beer now . . .

He goes to the kitchen.

Ned   Look at it this way . . . What you've got to understand is, that it's not the weapon that 'kills' people. It's the military strategist who's aiming it. Dan?

Dan *returns with beers.*

Ned   It's presidents and prime ministers and military commanders who decide these things . . . At the end of the day how they use it is not my responsibility. (*Beat.*) What are you looking at me like that for?

Dan *opens a beer, drinks.*

Dan   Like what?

Ned   Like – funny. You keep giving me funny looks. What are you giving me funny looks for?

Dan   I just think . . . Why didn't you tell me all this before?

Ned   I don't tell you everything. It's a secret.

Dan   But I'm your brother.

Ned   Well, I've told you now so shut the fuck up about it.

Ned *drinks.*

Dan *drinks.*

Silence.

Does Mum know?

Ned   What's it got to do with her?

Dan   I just think she might like to know about this.

Ned   She's not interested in this.

Dan   What do you mean?

Ned   She's not interested.

Dan   You mean, what, she doesn't want to talk about it?

Ned   What do you think?

Dan   You can't really blame her. I mean, this is . . . this . . . just . . . I don't even know what this is. It's beyond comprehension.

Ned   I suppose.

Dan   What does Janie think about it?

Ned   What do you think she thinks?

Dan   Well, are you surprised?

Ned   Not any more, no.

Ned *drinks.*

Dan *drinks.*

Ned   Mum hasn't rung me in ages. Janie won't talk about it without getting visibly upset.

Dan   Is this why she . . . ?

Ned   It's complicated. She just, you know, just . . . She's her own woman. She gets very emotional about it.

Silence.

Just, do me a favour, don't tell anybody else about this.

Dan   Who am I going to tell?

Ned   You mustn't tell Nancy.

Dan   Why can't I tell Nancy?

Ned   Why do you want to tell Nancy?

Dan   I tell her everything.

Ned   Why do you want to tell her about this?

Dan   Because I just think she might be interested.

Ned   Don't tell Nancy – you know what she's like, she'll just go on about the war and killing people and, you know, all the suffering little children and all that shit.

Dan   She's just got strong beliefs.

Ned   Well, I don't want to debate them with her so just leave it.

Dan   I might have to tell her.

Ned   Why?

Dan   I might need to confide in someone. I feel the need to confide in someone.

Ned   I feel the same way – but I signed the Official Secrets Act. It's classified technology. If you really need to confide, you can confide in me – or confide in Janie.

Dan   I'm not confiding in *your* wife – I want to confide in mine.

Ned   Just don't confide in anybody! OK?

Silence.

I didn't think you'd feel so strongly about it.

Silence.

Are your kids allowed to play with toy guns yet?

Dan   It's nothing to do with me, it's Nancy's decision. It's a bit neuro, I suppose, but she has a point.

Ned   'Neuro'?

Dan   Neurotic.

Ned   Then why does she have a point?

Dan   You don't have kids yet, perhaps if you did you might not do what you do.

Ned (*beat*)   What do you mean?

Dan   I mean you'd find it quite hard to explain probably.

Ned   You think so, do you?

Dan   I – I'd like to think so . . . You'd certainly think twice about it . . . wouldn't you?

Ned   Try explaining Botox to your kids, see what they say. Go on, it'll be a laugh.

Silence.

Are you hungry?

Dan   Eh?

Ned   Are you hungry?

Dan   No, I don't feel well . . . I think I need to lie down . . .

Ned   It's just the heat, you'll feel better with some lunch inside you.

Dan   No, I really do, I really feel really unwell . . .

Ned   Just pull yourself together . . . how do you think I feel?

Dan   I have no idea, Ned, no idea whatsoever how you feel, I couldn't begin to guess what goes through your mind.

Ned *drinks.*

Dan *just lolls about looking ill.*

Ned   What about the noodles?

Dan   What about them?

Ned   I thought we were going to have lunch?

Dan   No. I'm not hungry any more. I just told you.

Lights down.

Two

Ross, *dressed businesslike, stands in the middle of the room, holding an attaché case.*

Ross   This is nice. I love these high ceilings. And the cornice. And the rose. And that fireplace. Where did you get the fireplace? I've just bought a place in Somerset with my husband, an old farmhouse, and we're looking to install one of these. There's an existing wood-burning stove . . .

Ned *comes in with a coffee plunger and two cups. He pours as she talks.*

Ross   Bit of a walk from the tube. Very tucked away. Nice and high up, though. Nice view. You can smell the canal.

Ned   Drains, probably.

Ross No, it's nice, fresh . . . it's so warm . . . it's such a lovely day . . .

She undoes a button on her blouse – but not in a provocative way.

Oh! I'm so hot and sticky!

He eyes her warily.

Sorry, it's just so nice to be out of the office . . .

Ned No, you make yourself at home.

Ross I get cabin fever . . . I get really smelly . . . I go mental on the weekend.

Ned Let your hair down.

Ross I hate the M25! It's so depressing! I just want to stab somebody!

Ned Uh-huh . . .

Ross *noses about.*

Ross You're so lucky to have this place. It's a gold mine.

Ned I'm just renting.

Ross You're so lucky.

Ned *hands her a cup of coffee.*

Ned Do you want the grand tour?

Ross Oh no, I'm not being nosy. (*She sips.*) Good schools? I mean around here. Do you have kids?

Ned Not yet, no.

Ross Changes everything. Your entire life as you know it, out the window. Gone. It is gone. Kaput. Oh God. You won't know you're born! Little runts! (*Beat.*) But you know, they're great. They're really funny . . . personally it was very important to us that the children were funny or at least, you know, not stupid . . . I thought you lived in Kilburn for some reason.

Ned   That was years ago.

Ross   Kilburn's nice.

Ned   No it's not, it's a dump.

Ross   Oh no, it's lovely now. Nice restaurants, cheese shops, theatres . . .

Ned   Yeah. Everybody needs cheese shops and theatres . . .

They sip coffee.

Ross   I'm a huge fan of your work, I've been following your career, it's very impressive – and I have to say I am particularly excited about this.

Ned   OK, but –

Ross   No, I mean it. You've had such a good year. I mean, if you're really into guided weaponry, which I really really am, then this is a huge breakthrough.

Ned   If you know anything about this, you'll already know where I stand.

Ross *eyes a design on his laptop computer.*

Ross   That's pretty. What is it?

Ned   It's a jet.

Ross   A jet? No.

Ned   It opens and closes to control the temperature of the metal.

Ross   It's a work of art.

Ned   I like it, I'm really proud of it, actually, I've incorporated a lot of . . .

He goes quiet, studies his hands.

Ross   Go on. I'm interested.

He tilts the laptop to show the design at a better angle.

Ned   I used a lot of principles from Islamic, er, geometric art . . .

They examine the design.

Ross   I think it's glorious. How does it work?

Ned   This is just a primary circle with a natural sixfold division . . . one, two, three, see? If you move a compass point to the adjacent petals to cut off the arcs which intersect the first pair, you end up with twelve equal parts. When it's coloured the upright cross represents the solar equinoxes and solstices. It's also the twelve signs of the zodiac . . .

Ross   Fascinating . . .

Ned   OK, so these petals open and close to cool the metal. They sort of breathe . . . like a flower opening and closing at dawn and at dusk . . . Anyway, is this interesting?

Ross   You see, this is what I love about your stuff. It's so eclectic. It's like, where does it all come from? Your brain must be enormous . . .

Ned   I dunno . . . just one of my little obsessions.

Ross   I think all geniuses are a little bit obsessive . . .

Ned (*beat*)   'Geniuses . . . ' Huh.

Ross   It's like the programme. You take something very beautiful – bees, birds, solar equinox – and you make this extraordinary machinery . . . like da Vinci.

He stares at her a moment.

Ned   Actually, it is a bit. That's what I like to think.

Ross   The flying machine.

Ned   Yeah, yes, that sort of thing . . .

Ross (*excited*)   You know, he invented all sorts of weapons . . .

Ned   Yeah . . . I know . . .

Ross   Archimedes . . . 'The iron claw . . . '

Ned   Yeah, I know . . . the parabolic mirror – the first ever death ray.

Ross   The first ever defence contract with the government. They set him up with his own weapons lab. Imagine that.

Ned   Yeah . . . imagine.

He eyes her uncertainly as she studies the drawing. After a moment he shuts the laptop.

Ross   Hey, listen, I know you're unhappy and I know it's taking a long time to negotiate, but I just want to reassure you that it's nothing insidious . . .

Ned   Uh-huh . . .

Ross   There's just a slight capability issue.

Ned   I know all about the capability issue.

Ross   The MoD just wants a little extra hardware in the electronics bay . . .

Ned   And?

Ross   And more symbology for the weapon systems operator . . .

Ned   Why?

Ross   It's a usability issue. If the human–machine interface is questionable –

Ned   The human–machine interface?

Ross   We're selling this on usability.

Ned   Selling it?

Ross   To the MoD.

Ned   We're not 'selling' it to them . . .

Ross   No, but I mean, I have to sell them on it . . . it's a figure of speech.

Ned   OK . . .

Ross   And safety is critical. If people find it too difficult to use, mistakes could be deadly.

Ned   It's meant to be deadly.

Ross   You know what I mean –

Ned   Funny how people always worry about the machine's capability but never the human's . . .

Ross   How do you mean?

Ned   I'm saying – they always find the machine lacking – never the people using it. What if it's too easy to use? Have you ever thought of that?

Ross (*beat*)   I don't understand what you mean.

Ned   Do we want this to be so easy to use that any old bunch of dummies can fire it? It's not Space Invaders.

Ross   What do you mean?

Ned   It's precision technology. It *should* be difficult to use.

Ross   All they want is an indicator to show which weapon is selected.

Ned   If they don't know which weapon they've selected, then they shouldn't be operating it.

Ross   Please, listen, and I'll explain. I know capability like playing hardball, but –

Ned   They're saying it's not up to scratch?

Ross   Not in the slightest, far from it in fact. What they're saying is –

Ned   The government will only finance it if we stick all this junk in the electronics bay so they can put it in a fancy brochure and flog it at the next weapons fair?

Ross   I'm saying there's a capability issue, but the Capability People have been speaking to the Requirement People –

Ned   Requirements?

Ross   Yes – and they actually like it.

Ned (*beat*)   They 'like it'.

Ross   They say it's all there. It's spare, but it's there. It's not a problem.

Ned   And the avionics?

Ross   They like 'em. Not a problem.

Pause.

Ned   OK. So . . . so what do they really want?

Ross   Why do you assume they want anything?

Ned   Everybody wants something. Everybody wants me to change something for them. They're like dogs pissing on a post just so that it smells of them.

Pause.

Ross   OK. They're assuming it's going to be compatible with America's global positioning system.

Pause.

Ned   Why?

Ross   Why do you think?

Ned   And if Europe develops a better global positioning system?

Ross   We still make it compatible with America. We've been developing it with American engineers . . .

Ned   Yeah, well, I've had a few thoughts on that . . .

Ross   What d'you mean?

Ned   Do we want America to have control of this technology simply because they control global positioning? If we develop a better GPS in Europe, isn't it better that we control the technology?

Ross   We have no intention of letting them control it.

Ned   Well then, it has to be compatible with European GPS. There's every chance it'll be bigger and better than America's. If they want to use this, they'll have to use ours.

Pause.

Ross   Ned, there's a question of loyalty here . . . The Americans have been loyal and cooperative and helpful. They're tenacious and determined and savvy and we need them on board.

Ned   I appreciate all that . . . but this is an opportunity to . . . change a lot of things.

Ross   What do you want to change?

Ned   Well . . . um . . . ha ha . . . Well, there's a question.

Ross   It's not funny, what are you trying to change? I don't want to change anything. I'm happy just the way things are.

Ned (*beat*)   I'm just pointing out that in a few years' time, European GPS technology will be better than America's . . . and if we're savvy about it, we can take advantage of that . . .

Ross   What's 'savvy' about it?

Ned   We own the intellectual property . . . it's our prerogative.

Ross   Well, in actual fact we don't entirely own the intellectual property . . . If you look at the contract . . .

She opens her attaché case. She hands over a copy of the contract. He reads.

The MoD will split the intellectual property with the factory . . .

Ned   And with the Americans? Is that what you're saying?

Ross   The MoD will fund the prototype, it'll fund the new trials, it'll fund manufacture . . .

Ned (*dawning realisation*)   And split the IP with the Americans . . . That's why it has to be compatible with American GPS? They're going to split it with the Yanks?

Ross   Not the military. Just the engineers. The MoD thinks it's right that they're granted a small share in exchange for their contribution to development.

Ned   Whaaat? We had a contract. They were contracted to to to . . . there was never a question of granting them . . . Are you serious?

Ross   OK, calm down . . .

Ned   It's not what was agreed.

Ross   We'll get you a royalty.

Ned   You mean you'll split a royalty.

Ross   We pool all royalties.

Ned   I don't want to pool my royalties.

Ross   A royalty pool. Everybody has to pool.

Ned   Well, I'm not pooling. I don't want to pool.

Ross   You'll be on points. You'll have points in the pool.

Ned   Who else is in the pool?

Ross   The MoD owns the pool. The Yanks get a dip. It's standard practice.

Ned stares. *He glares at the contract again.*

Ned   OK, well, what will you give me to ensure I don't quit and start my own company? What will you give me to remain loyal?

Ross   If we absolutely have to? If you're intent on pushing us. 'Sweat equity.'

Ned   'Sweat equity.'

Ross   We'll pay for all your sweat – you just need to get a patent. But you won't get a patent because it's not solely your work. You couldn't have done it without the Americans. Collectively we were able to do something which individually . . .

Ned   Very funny . . . very clever . . . Touché . . .

Ross   You would have to build a good 'business case'.

Ned   A 'business case . . . '

Ross   Or you could just sign this contract now and part ownership is yours.

She produces a pen.

Ned   What's the percentage? (*Pause.*) What is it?

Ross   The MoD wants fifty-one per cent –

Ned   A controlling share!

Ross   To pay for manufacture. They'll fund manufacture – capped at seventy million when we recoup.

Ned   Capped?

Ross   Capped at seventy million – that's the beauty. They put in seventy million, we cap the payback at seventy million, not a penny more. It's like a-a-a – an interest-free loan, it's terrific.

Ned   They agreed to a cap?

Ross   I always cap. I believe in capping. I'm a capper.

Ned   So the MoD controls it but they can't prof— they can't profit from it?

Ross   They can't profit from *us*.

Ned   Then who?

Ross   They have to export to America to make their profit. That's when the royalties kick in.

Ned (*beat, stares*)   And and and and and what will the Americans do with it? Export it to someone else?

Ross (*beat*)   Only if our government licenses it – no, listen – licenses it for re-export and if it's required by another ally . . .

Ned   Uh-huh . . . Which ally? Israel? The Saudis?

Ross (*beat*)   Who knows?

Ned   Well, somebody knows . . .

Ross   Sure, yeah, it's a question that's bound to be asked . . .

Ned   Well, I'm asking it. Is it possible?

Ross (*beat*)   Anything's possible . . .

Ned   Well, this is what I'm getting at. When I started this programme, Israel had pulled out of Lebanon . . . there was no war in Iraq . . . the world was was was . . .

Ross   Well, you know perfectly well we can't develop anything without American help . . . we just don't have the infrastructure –

Ned   Well, that's what worries me . . .

Ross   We don't have the infrastructure because we don't have the *commitment* –

Ned   What have I been *doing* – ?

Ross   You were just trying to negotiate yourself a royalty!

Ned   I deserve a royalty because it's *mine* – I drafted plans from scratch. I 'invented' it. Conjured out of thin air!

Ross   But 'you' actually didn't, not on your own.

Ned   Well, I would dispute that . . .

Ross   Clearly the mechanics are yours. The avionics aren't.

Ned   I came up with the the the *rules* . . . the *rules* for the the – I'm happy to go through page by page what I contributed and what the Americans helped with . . .

Ross   In your judgement. In your opinion. Of course they disagree.

Ned   I brought the idea to you. We contracted the Americans.

Ross   We *commissioned* you. We commissioned the Americans. Which suggests it was *our* idea to commission.

Ned   You don't even know how it works!

Ross   It's not my job!

Ned   I'll show you the plans –

Ross   As Commercial Director – there's the clue – 'commercial' –

Ned   I drew up –

Ross   My job –

Ned   Bef—

Ross   My job is –

Ned   But bef—

Ross   To sell.

Ned   Before I even discussed –

Ross   How many people were working on swarming? *Everybody.*

Ned (*beat, stares*)   I'll take it to arbitration.

Ross   You can arbitrate until you're blue in the face, but this is *venture capitalism* – everything the government does is venture capitalism – from weapons of mass destruction to school dinners. They'll screw you till your teeth drop out. Which is why I want to be *across* this. Which is why I'm here now *negotiating* with you. For your sake. It's for your sake.

Ned *stares.*

Ross   So what do you want? Do you want a royalty or do you want to make a point?

Ned *stares.*

Silence.

Ross   All right, look, even if it was . . . eventually sold to a few people . . . to Israel . . . by the Americans . . . certainly not by us . . . it's a sovereign nation, we can't tell the Israelis what to do with their weapons any more than Russia can. (*Pause.*) Obviously the Israelis are desperate for weaponised UAVs. They could use them on the West Bank – which I might add is heavily reliant on American GPS and is in itself a very lucrative market –

Ned   I know all about that, I was at the weapons fair . . .

Ross   The Russians sold rockets to Iran and the very next day sold to Israel the technology to shoot them down. They're more entrepreneurial than the rest of us put together. The best thing about this is, it's a powerful bargaining tool −

Ned   Bargaining − for what? World peace?

Ross (*beat*)   Well . . . You know, Ned . . . I think this is a rather distasteful conversation which we probably shouldn't even be having. It's not my job to speculate and it's certainly not yours.

Ned   It's not speculation. This is going to change everything. We'd better know what we're doing.

Ross   What did you think was going to happen? Did you really think you could work with American engineers but not the American military? Did you really think the government would fund it without wanting to control it?

Ned   I thought we could try . . . try and use the thing to to to . . . I thought this might be different.

Ross   It's never different. It's just different . . . foreplay.

She offers him the pen.

Go on. You know you want to.

She pokes him with the pen.

It'll be fun. (*Mouths the words.*) Go on . . .

Ned (*beat*)   I'll have to think very carefuly about this . . .

Ross   Are you hungry? I could murder a curry.

Ned   You think because I'm an engineer, I'll roll over for a curry?

They look at each other.

Lights down.

Three

Dan *is at the table with a takeaway curry. He dishes up the takeaway.*

Ned (*off*)   Do you know what a 'paradigm shifter' is?

Dan   Is it to do with trigonometry?

Ned (*off*)   A paradigm shifter is an invention that changes the rules of the game. Fire was the first paradigm shifter. The wheel, the internet, computers, liquid paper, the Beatles and the atomic bomb . . .

He comes in with cans of beer, hands one to **Dan**.

Ned   They all changed the landscape in such a way that everything was different and there was no going back. The burning question is always, how's it going to be used? How's it going to change things? Is it the beginning . . . or the end?

Dan   So you obviously have qualms . . .

Ned   Eh?

Dan   *Qualms*. You have *qualms*.

Ned   'Qualms'? Oh yeah, sure, everybody has qualms . . . But I'll overcome them. I'm just using them as − (*cracks open beer*) leverage.

Dan (*cracks open beer*)   'Leverage' for what?

Ned   To do the deal that I want to do.

Dan   So you're still going ahead with . . . ahead with it?

Ned   Well, I haven't signed anything yet but, yeah. I just want to do it my way.

Dan   Because, you know, it's it's it's a hell of a responsibility . . .

Ned   Well, Dan, a Russian named Mikhail Kalashnikov invented the Kalashnikov but it doesn't mean every time someone uses a Kalashnikov he's responsible. He didn't know what people were going to do with it.

Dan   It's a gun. What did he think they would do with it?

Ned   He thought they'd defend their homes and their families.

Dan   Well, that's OK then . . .

Ned   Don't you think people have the right to defend themselves against suicide bombers seeking martyrdom?

Dan   Sort of . . .

Ned *goes to the kitchen, returns with a huge knife from the knife block.* **Dan** *eyes the knife uneasily.*

Ned   See this?

Dan (*extremely doubtful*)   Mm . . .

Ned   Many different uses. I can chop vegetables, I can throw it at a target, or I can just cut your head off with it. The fact that I can cut your head off with it doesn't mean they should stop making them. What would you use to cook with? (*Beat.*) What if some axe-wielding homicidal maniac breaks in during the night? It's a great deterrent. The governments which we deal with favour a strategy of defence. It's called 'defence' because it's about defending from attack.

He drives the knife into a wooden bread board with a vicious 'thunk'.

Pause.

Dan   And attacking.

Ned   What do you mean?

Dan   It's about defending *and* attacking.

Ned   Well, they do say 'attack is the best form of defence'.

Dan   But that knife wasn't designed to attack people.

Ned   It's adaptable. What we call in the weapons industry 'dual use'. Like nuclear power. Can be a weapon, doesn't have to be.

Dan   I don't understand how you can equivocate.

Ned   Maybe I have to. What if there's another world war? Not the 'war on terror', a proper one. What they call 'a just war'. What if there's another Hitler intent on invading us and making us all into Nazis?

Dan   Don't you think we should cross that bridge when we come to it?

Ned   No, we need to be ready. When Hitler was bombing the factories in Shepherd's Bush what do you think our grandparents were thinking? Do you think they were thinking, 'Ooh dear, what are we going to do? We don't want to hurt anybody. I hope those poor Spitfire pilots don't do anything silly because we don't want any trouble. We're ideologically opposed to violence. Violence is bad.' Were they thinking that? No. They were thinking, 'Let's kill everybody in the fucking Luftwaffe before they kill us because we want to have children and grandchildren one day, like normal people. Stop these evil Nazi fucks now or so help us God we'll be barbecued alive in our beds.' And they weren't warmongers. They weren't reactionaries. They just wanted it to stop, and the only way it was going to stop was if somebody stopped them.

He sits, resumes eating.

Dan *drinks.*

Dan   OK, so . . . bear with me here . . . what happens if they use it for an 'unjust war'? Or or or or or or at least a, you know, an 'illegal' one?

Ned   I don't really want to get into what's 'just' or 'unjust' . . . with you. Illegal and unjust are not the same things . . . (*Pause.*) Obviously Iraq was illegal, but that's the way it's done now – it's a a a completely new military morality.

Dan *stares, fork halfway to mouth.*

Ned   Hey – I know it's, you know, evil-and-bad-and-sick-and-twisted but the world is full of bad, bad people, Dan. An' if they weren't so frigging *bad*, we wouldn't have to kill them. (*Long pause.*) Don't look at me like that! It's true!

Dan   Who decides who's bad and who's not bad? You?

Ned   OK, listen, obviously I'm being a bit facetious. But what are the alternatives? The government has fallen in love with nuclear weapons again – North Korea has them, Iran wants them. War in the Middle East isn't going to go away in our lifetime, it just isn't, privately this is widely accepted in the government . . . I don't like the idea of selling my ideas to America or Israel any more than you do but . . . you know . . . maybe it's a weapon they *should* be using. Maybe we need a completely new paradigm for weapons . . . *unmanned* weapons . . . *unmanned* battlefields. No human combatants.

Dan *just stares at him, vaguely appalled.*

Dan   A 'new paradigm for weapons' . . . ?

Ned   . . . for a new military morality.

Dan   No human combatants?

Ned   It's right around the corner.

Dan   You mean . . . you mean no human *allies*. The *enemy* will still be human. We'll still be killing *them*.

Ned (*thinks, beat*)   Listen, it's really pretty simple: if people are no longer prepared to obey 'rules of war' and are prepared to – to put it bluntly – kill innocent civilians . . . I have a responsibility to take that into account. With my technology, if the intelligence is good, it's impossible to hit the wrong target.

Dan   What if the intelligence is, you know, 'bad'?

Ned   Well . . . see . . . this puts the onus on the intelligence agencies to just, you know, pull their socks up a bit . . .

Dan   Good plan, Ned, that should do the trick.

Ned   It'll revolutionise warfare because it's very hard to hit the wrong target . . . it's very hard to kill innocent civilians.

Dan   What if they *choose* to hit the wrong targets?

Ned   Well . . . well, listen . . . I have to assume that isn't going to happen.

Dan   It happens all the time.

Ned   OK, look . . . all the allies find it hard when this kind of thing happens. But what you have to understand is, when a drone targets a school bus, it's not targeting it because it's a school bus. It's probably just targeting Scud launchers. It just so happens that Scud launchers have the same spec and shape and size as a school bus.

Dan   The same 'spec'?

Ned   Specifications. Military personnel will always explain it as a mistake. And usually they're telling the truth.

Dan   Wait a minute – how is it a mistake?

Ned   I just told you.

Dan   No – wait a minute –

Ned   It really is.

Dan   No – just – *no*. This is a mistake – (*Knocks his empty glass over.*) See? I made a mistake, I didn't see it there, whoopsie, I won't make that mistake again. Now, correct me if I'm wrong, but that's not the same as an Apache helicopter vaporising an entire family running for their lives in the family sedan.

Ned   If you'll let me finish: the problem is not that mistakes are made, the problem is that they're gung-ho enough to keep making them.

Dan   'Gung-ho'? You see, this is where you leave me behind: the terminology.

Ned   Just – stop being pedantic.

Dan   Well, I happen to think that a little more 'pedantry' would go a long way.

Ned   What this weapon does is, it forces governments to eradicate mistakes – no, don't laugh – I'm trying to teach you something about the way the world really works. The real world, for real, in real life.

Dan   Well . . . I can't argue with you when you're like this. You were in America too long. What did they give you to make you so loyal? The world's largest cheeseburger?

He plays with his food.

Ned   I happen to be putting my balls on the line to stop America gaining a monopoly on this technology.

Dan   Don't you think it's a bit late for that? Jesus . . . this is, this is disastrous . . . they're a bad influence.

He pushes his plate away, gets up.

Ned   You sound like Mum now.

Dan   I *feel* like Mum sometimes. I'm horrified by the possibilities . . . (*Beat.*) I need a piss.

Ned   I need one too.

He gets up. **Dan** *makes a move for the bathroom –* **Ned** *makes a move.* **Dan** *gestures.*

Ned   We'll both go . . . we can have swordfights.

Dan *ignores this, goes into the bathroom, pisses with the door open.*

Ned   It's my job. And it has been for some time now, so there's not much I can do about it now.

Dan (*off*)   You were designing aircraft parts. Testing them in wind tunnels in Wales, going up in jets. What a great job. I was jealous.

He flushes and returns.

I was talking to an oral surgeon the other day . . . He has a young soldier who's come back from Iraq with half his face blown off. All he wants is a shepherd's pie and to kiss his girfriend on the lips . . . and he can't because he hasn't even got a gullet . . . He'll have the entire World Cup squad in his mouth by now – cranio-facial, temporomandibular, a prosthodontist – he'll need dentures – Who wants to make falsies for a nineteen-year-old? There's soldiers coming home now with injuries so horrific and strange we don't even know what weapon was used.

They stare at each other.

Ned   I want to finish the programme, Dan . . . I have to get this thing made . . . It's what I do . . . It's my life. Otherwise it's just theoretical . . . pointless . . . a recipe without any of the ingredients . . .

Dan   Well . . . I can see it's a great opportunity . . .

Ned   Exactly . . . This is, you know, the cutting edge of technology . . . this is where the best technology comes from.

Dan   But you don't know what this thing will do to people.

Ned   The whole point about weapons is they're empirical. You don't know exactly what they'll do until you use them. You hope it's the solution, you hope it's not going to be too ugly, but you can't prove it until you try it.

Dan   And what if it just makes things worse?

Ned   I have to try . . . If I don't, I'll never design anything else again . . . I'll go mad.

Dan   Well, I'll go mad if you do.

Ned   Don't say that.

Dan   Nancy would sooner butcher the kids than support this kind of thing.

Ned   Well, where do you stand on butchering the kids?

Dan   Ned . . .

Ned   Nancy's a loony.

Dan   I know she's a loony, but she's entitled to her beliefs.

Ned   Oh fuck Nancy and her beliefs. She's a bully. You only married her because she put a gun to your head.

Dan (*beat*)   Wh— ? That's not true!

Ned   She got you in a headlock and threatened to leave you if you didn't inseminate her.

Dan   You better watch yourself here.

Ned   She bullied you into having kids and then she bullied them into not having water pistols. Too bad when they find out what Uncle Ned does for a living.

Dan   Maybe they won't find out.

Ned   You mean, maybe you won't tell them? Maybe I'll tell them.

Dan   Maybe you won't be around to tell them. If you're going to behave like this.

Ned   Oho! You're going to ban me from seeing your kids? My own niece and nephew? Nobody does that. It's ridiculous.

Dan   It's not because of what you do –

Ned   It's not?

Dan   It's because of who you are.

Ned   Who am I?

Dan (*beat*)   I don't want to get into that now.

Ned   Who are you? Prancing around Shepherd's Bush in a Jeep, sticking people's faces full of rat poison so you can buy a fucking swimming pool!

Dan   I do a lot to ease people's pain . . . At least I contribute to people's lives and not to their fucking deaths!

Ned *throws his glass of water at* **Dan**.

Dan *stands, open-mouthed, shocked.*

Dan   You *baby*! What did you do that for?

Ned   I don't expect many people to understand, but I expect my own family to.

Dan   What do you think Dad would say?

Ned (*beat*)   He would have understood.

Dan   D'you think so? Really? If he was here now, he'd –

Ned   All right all right, I get the message!

Dan   He would roll in his grave!

Ned *stares intensely, hurt.*

Ned   Well, as long as he doesn't roll out of it and come and see me at work I'll live with it.

Dan *gets a tea towel, mops the wet table and clears the spoiled food.*

Dan   You've ruined my curry. You invited me. I didn't invite myself. Do you think I was thinking, 'Hmm, I really need to get around to Ned's with a takeaway so he can hector me about the military – I love it when he's condescending?' No. I was thinking, 'Ned's lonely, it's Friday, he needs company – what a pain in the arse!' (*Clearing, cleaning*) You're an incredibly annoying, very difficult, rather strange person – I don't know if you're aware of it. I'm not surprised Janie left if this is how you behave at home . . .

Ned   Dan, would you just stop going on about her?

Dan   Not at all surprised . . .

Ned   What would you do in my position? What would you do? Apart from resigning and buying supplies for your next expedition to the moral high ground. You could stand at the summit with Nancy wringing your hands and sucking each other's dicks.

Dan *throws his glass of water at* **Ned**.

Beat.

Ned   You cunt.

He throws a container of rice at **Dan**.

Beat.

Dan *grabs* **Ned** *by the shirt and yanks him close.*

Dan   Take back what you said about Nancy.

Ned   Don't fuck with me, Dan. I'm warning you, I am the last person in the world you want to fuck with right now.

They wrestle over the table, food and glasses etc. go flying.

Eventually **Ned** *gets the upper hand and wrestles* **Dan** *onto the table, rolling him about in the food, wrestling wordlessly.*

Then **Dan** *gets the upper hand. He somehow flips* **Ned** *over and now* **Ned** *is rolling about in the food.*

During all this they say nothing, only grunting a little, but really concentrating too intently to make much noise.

Eventually they run out of steam, stop, stand up. They stare at each other.

There's a strange buzzing sound, **Ned***'s mobile phone is vibrating on the table. He lets it go for a while, then picks it up anxiously.*

Ned   Hello? Oh, hi . . . No, I was just . . . finishing my . . . curry . . . Uh, jalfrezi . . . Yes, it was very nice . . . No, I'm still . . . No, well, I think . . . Well, I think . . . I know . . . I know . . . I know . . . I know . . . I didn't know that. *(Pause.)* Well, I'm perfectly serious about that . . . In fact I'm . . .

Pause. **Ned** *shoots* **Dan** *a look.*

Ned   I've changed my mind . . . I don't want to talk about it . . . I've thought about it and I've made my decision . . . I can't go throught with it . . . I can't go ahead with this agreement . . . I'm sorry.

Ned *snaps the phone shut.*

They look at each other.

Blackout.

Act Two

One

Aircraft factory.

Ross *has a contract.* **Ned** *is standing around, nervous.*

The ear-splitting roar of a jet engine is heard outside.

They wait for the noise to subside.

Ross   It's OK, I understand. You think you've had some kind of epiphany and now you're pure . . . You *believe* . . . It's not about dirty filthy lucre . . . and so on . . .

Ned   It's not about money.

Ross   How much do you want?

Ned (*beat*)   It's not about that.

Ross   Well, if we start making this, somebody's going to make a lot of money.

Ned   I don't give a shit about the money.

Ross   Well, you should, because apart from anything else this factory is one of the biggest employers in the country. Like it or not, defence is a growth industry. The local area around here is depending on us for millions of pounds' worth of regeneration – no, listen – just as it did after the Second World War when the country was in ruins. This whole neighbourhood was in ruins, in fact. If you renege on us and the bottom falls out of the market, I hope you're prepared to explain yourself to the community . . .

Ned   Well . . . I'm sorry about the neighbourhood, but it's what I believe is right.

Ross   It's not right, it's just selfish. We have bills to pay. Taxes to pay. Wages to distribute. You have responsibilities to your colleagues and to your family and to yourself. What will you do if we stop now? You'll go mad. You won't be able to live with yourself. It's my future too. I have a family to feed. I have children. School fees. A mortgage. This is my livelihood. This is normal life for normal people trying to do an honest day's work and just make ends meet.

Pause.

Ned   I'm sorry but I can't . . . in all good conscience –

Ross   Don't talk to me about your 'conscience' . . . That's just moral exhibitionism.

Ned   What do you expect me to –

Ross   We have an IP –

Ned   Do you want me to lie?

Ross   We have an IP –

Ned   And say, 'Good idea, well done' –

Ross   – *Lawyer* –

Ned   'A blow for the free market?'

Ross   – who has asked me –

Ned   I'm not interested in your lawyer –

Ross   – to point out, if –

Ned   I can't sign that.

Ross   – if –

Ned   I've change my mind.

Ross   – if you read your employment contract, you will see that under the conditions of your employment you are required to make 'best endeavours' to get projects financed. Best endeav—

Ned   This is ridic—

Ross   Not 'reasonable endeavours'. Not, you'll 'think about it'. Or you've 'changed your mind'.

Ned   This is different. I think we should go back to the drawing board. Talk to the French or the Germans.

Ross   Well – you see – OK – well – we can't. Because – let me explain – if it weren't for this funding, if we don't start manufacture next year, there will be no 'drawing board'. Your ideas will be worthless. And . . . if it weren't for this government and our partnership with the Americans you would have no acolytes and no support. You would be nowhere. A jobbing engineer. Studying the flight of birds and bees? People would laugh at you. They'd say you were stupid.

Pause.

Ned   So I don't have a choice?

Ross   I don't understand what's got your back up all of a sudden . . .

Ned   You love my work so much that you're offering me powerlessness.

Ross   But when it comes to lucrative government contracts, we were always offering you powerlessness. I'm bending over backwards to offer you a *deal* . . . OK? A deal to ensure you retain a percentage of your intellectual property . . .

Ned (*beat, thinks*)   No. A percentage? No. I need the whole lot. It's it's it's all or nothing . . .

Ross (*snorts*)   We love you, Ned, but we're not going to humour you for ever.

Ned   I need full ownership of the patent in order to control the export licence.

Ross   Why would you want to do that?

Ned   Because the only way I can see of this working . . . is if I control the export licence.

Ross   We'll control the export licence, you just, don't worry your pretty little head –

Ned   No, the government will control the export licence and you know what they'll do with it –

Ross   If you go to the government saying you want finance but you want to control the export licence they'll think you're a demented control freak!

Ned   It takes one to know one!

Ross   And if America wanted to re-export the damned thing they could reclassify it 'dual use'.

Ned   So you're absolving yourself of responsibility?

Ross   I'm saying there are *regulations* to absolve us of responsibility.

Ned   Well, don't you think that's kind of *fishy*?

Pause.

Ross   Listen. OK, I'll put my cards on the table. The government will never let us own a controlling share. They won't compromise. They'll just let it wilt on the vine.

Ned   What do you mean?

Ross   You see, what's also important here is industry. And what matters to industry is *ownership*.

Ned   What matters to industry is profit.

Ross   Be That As It May. The government needs to hold on to this. Develop it or not develop it, leave it on the shelf, bury it, suffocate it, whatever – but it's got to remain their property. So that nobody else can exploit it . . . because that would be disastrous. That would be an economic nightmare.

Pause.

Ned   You're saying they they they . . . they might not even make it anyway?

Ross   Not unless they have a controlling share.

Ned   They're just going to sit on it? For for for economic reasons? This is like a bad dream. It just gets worse and worse. You're just . . . (*Pause.*) You're saying you'll just . . . It's a Military Requirement!

Ross   Nevertheless: the Ministry of Defence cannot be relied upon to see it through. It can be relied upon when it comes to anti-submarine aircraft which will never be used, or 'bomb-proof' Land Rovers which aren't even bullet-proof – but something as complex and esoteric as this will almost certainly go by the wayside. And as far as the Ministry of Defence is concerned . . . if we let you finish it and we also let you own it, then you take it to *somebody else* . . .

Ned   I wouldn't . . . I wouldn't!

Ross   And some other European country manufactures it . . . and then that country becomes the world's biggest arms manufacturer and they have the billions of euros in trade and the sinecures and the respect and the kudos that really belongs to us . . . do you see . . . they'll have all the fun and we'll go down the pipes and the defence industry will go the way of the motor industry and shipbuilding.

Ned   I wouldn't do that . . . I wouldn't.

Ross   You asked for 'sweat equity'! Nobody's going to give you 'sweat equity', they'll just get another designer. And look, I'll be bluntly honest with you here: obviously it would set us back a bit . . . it'll cost us . . . it's not ideal . . . but there's plenty of good designers willing to take over your work. You know that. There's people on your own team . . .

Ned   They wouldn't do that to me . . .

Ross   That's just vanity.

Ned   I don't believe you . . .

Ross   It's a great opportunity for someone.

Ned   There's nobody on that team who'd do that to me . . .

Ross   It's going to look great on someone's CV. And as for the royalties . . . royalties don't stop, they just keep on rolling in for ever.

Ned   I'm finding this a bit scary now.

He wanders a few steps, clears his head.

Ross   I'm not trying to scare you. Believe me. Scaring people is the last thing I want to achieve. (*Beat.*) But . . . what I will say is this. (*Beat.*) What happens if we quit and North Korea or Iran tries to develop one? (*Pause.*) If we acquire a patent, then only we can make it. If somebody manages to procure or develop one through clandestine means and they use it on us, then, having made it, we'll know how to stop it. If, on the other hand, we're seen to be developing weapons and then abandoning them when we get cold feet, this country will never be able to use weapons programmes as a deterrent again.

Ned   What happens if it doesn't work as a deterrent – what if it works as provocation?

Ross   If you don't finish, then it's an *invitation* for somebody else to.

Ned   What happens if we end up escalating the conflict? What happens if we incentivise Downing Street and the White House to continue waging illegal wars they can never win?

Pause.

Ross   I see. Well. OK. Great. Good. And and and you've been working on the programme for a good few years now, earning a nice wage while you're at it – when was the road to Damascus moment which slung it all into reverse for you? Was it when I told you it's actually going into production and it's no longer theoretical? And while we're on the subject of your hypocrisy: you sold it to us first.

Ned   What do you mean?

Ross   You're not just handing it over, for nothing, for free, it's not a gift. You offered us your time and expertise and your ideas and we paid you. That, in most people's books, constitutes a transaction, with a contract, whether you like it or not.

Ned   Well, I'm not most people.

Silence.

Ross's *mobile phone vibrates and she picks it up.*

Ross   Ross . . . (*Sweetly.*) Oh, hello! . . . I was just talking about you . . . Yes, I'm with him now . . .

Ned *pays attention.*

Ross   Well, I'm with him now . . . I can talk to him now . . . (*Pause.*) Really? Who said this? Really? Oh my goodness . . .

She eyes **Ned**, *alarming him.* **Ned** *fidgets uncomfortably, trying not to listen but unable to avoid it.*

Ross   Well, I can tell him now . . . if you're absolutely . . . if this is the only . . . (*Pause.*) No, it's no trouble . . . I don't mind at all . . . Absolutely . . . Well, absolutely . . . it's not my . . . Well, quite. Work out a . . . absolutely . . . (*Pause.*) Yes, I'm expecting . . . I'm expecting him . . . Send him over . . . Fabulous . . . No, not at all – it's a pleasure talking to you, as always.

She hangs up and puts away the contract in a briefcase.

Ok. (*Pause.*) There's been a development. (*Pause.*) I've been instructed not to renew your contract.

Ned   I never signed the contract.

Ross   I mean your contract of employment with the factory. They've decided to offer you redundancy. OK? They're making you redundant.

Pause.

Ned   Since when?

Ross   Since now. They've had enough.

Ned   You can't sack me. You must think I'm stupid . . .

Ross   I don't, actually. They do, but I like you.

Brooks *appears in the doorway.*

Ross (*to* **Brooks**)   That was quick.

Ned (*noticing* **Brooks** *but addressing* **Ross**)   What development? What have I . . . What am I meant to have done?!

Brooks   Is this a good time?

Ross   This is Mr Brooks from SIS. He's just popped in to help clarify a few things.

Ned   What've . . . what have I done?

Brooks *comes in.*

Brooks (*looking around*)   The Americans think you're a 'Jew-hater'.

Silence.

Ned *stares, shocked.*

Ned   I'm a-a-a . . . ?

Brooks   They think that you're anti-Semitic.

Ned   Which Americans?

Brooks   American Americans. In America. Not the Jewish lobby. New Testament God-fearing Republican blue-eyed boys. Clear-skinned, puritanical Bible-bashing descendants from the *Mayflower*, with an American flag and a basketball hoop in their front gardens and names like 'Peregrine'. In fact . . . I know a Peregrine in the CIA. You know what it means? It's a kind of hawk . . . the peregrine falcon.

Ned   . . . ?

Brooks   Weird, isn't it? It takes all sorts.

Ross   As they say in California, you're not a 'joiner'.

Brooks   Are you an atheist?

Ned   I I I I . . . what?

Brooks   Are you an atheist?

Ned   I'm agnostic . . .

Brooks   Now there's a word you don't hear any more . . . 'Agnostic'. From what I hear you're agnostic about a lot of things, aren't you?

Ned   Listen to me – I don't have a problem with –

Brooks   Well, they think you do.

Ned   I have Israeli friends −

Brooks   Congratulations.

Ned   In Tel Aviv −

Brooks   I'm really glad to hear it. What do you want, a medal?

Ned   I just don't think this programme . . . I don't think this is the solution . . . to to to their problems or to ours.

Brooks   Well, you'd know. You're the one with the friends in Tel Aviv. Have you ever been there?

Ned   No . . . but −

Brooks   Oh, you've never been there? Well, I have. Yeah. And I can tell you now they hate this sort of thing. They get it all the time . . . Everybody thinks they're poodles for America, can you imagine how annoying that is?

Pause.

Ned   OK, well . . . what is it they want me to do? They want me to sign this agreement? So they can have a-a-a share of the IP too?

Brooks   No. They don't want you to do anything now. They just want you to fuck off.

Ross   The Americans are very sensitive.

Brooks   Do you think you've stumbled on some big secret? Government monopoly of the arms trade − golly − what a scandal! Whoever heard of such a thing? Big deal.

Ned   It's a big deal to me . . .

Brooks   Then you're alone in the world. You are alone in the world on this one. Because you can have a dialogue with us about this any day of the week. It's no secret. In fact, the whole point is, when it was a secret, back in the day, when it was just, you know, the odd shipment of tanks to Indonesia . . .

people might have been shocked – because it was a secret. But you see, what we've done is really clever. We've started a dialogue about it. We have an open and friendly dialogue about everything from cluster-bombing to rendition. We have a good dialogue with the press, we're happy to be held accountable every now and then. Hell's bells, we release photographs of prisoners who are victims of civil rights abuse actually being abused on a fairly regular basis now. It shows we're cooperating. It reassures people. Do you follow what I'm trying to say?

Ned (*stares at* **Brooks**)   Who are you? I don't . . . I don't believe you're Military Intelligence or-or-or Secret Service or whoever the fuck you say you are.

Brooks (*shrugs*)   Why not?

Ned   You don't look like Intelligence. You don't talk like it either . . .

Brooks   Who were you expecting, Roger Moore?

Ned   Who is he? I thought you were 'across' this. You said you were 'across' . . . across . . .

He trails off. Beat.

Brooks   You're a pretty intense kind of guy, aren't you? I can tell. You boil at a different temperature . . . I like that.

Ned   'Brooks'? Is that your name?

Brooks   Call me Lenny.

Ned   'Lenny from Intelligence.' Right, so I can trust *you*.

Brooks   I'd like to think you can.

Ned   Well, I don't really think you know what you're talking about. If we start making this thing, your entire life is going to change, OK? Intelligence will be *everything*.

Brooks   Well, I actually think it already is.

Ned   The pressure, OK, on you guys to find targets and identify them one hundred per cent accurately with no mistakes . . . is going to increase exponentially –

Brooks   I like a challenge.

Ned   First and foremost this is surveillance technology –

Brooks   I love surveillance . . . it's the best bit. I love following people.

Ned   I think I'd like to go home now . . .

Brooks   It's going to be great.

Ross   We're in an impossible position. We have to break the deadlock.

Brooks   It's a Military Requirement.

Ross   A requirement issue, absolutely.

Ned   All the same, I can't work like this . . .

Ross   Well, I don't think you should go just yet.

Brooks   You can go home when we're finished.

Ned   Finished what?

Brooks   When we're done here. We all have homes to go to.

Ross   I've got to get home to my kids . . .

Brooks   Me too. I've got a little boy . . . he hates it when I'm late . . .

Silence.

And I'd nix the Islamic art if I were you. We know why you do it, but try explaining it to the Americans . . .

Ross   It's not the Islamic part, it's 'art' that freaks them out . . .

Brooks   That's right. A lot of people think artists are weirdos . . .

Ross   It sends out the wrong message.

Brooks   In a war, people destroy art and architecture to make a point. We do it because that kind of shit messes with their minds and hits them where it hurts.

Ned *looks from one to the other, increasingly alarmed.*

Ned   Do you really think this is the answer? This is the grand solution to to to all our problems?

Brooks   Yeah, sit down –

Ned   I'm not sitting, I'm not 'under arrest' –

Brooks   Not yet.

Ned   What are you talking about? You can't arrest me . . . what have I done?

Brooks   I'm joking! Relax. What are you so jumpy about? Why so nervous?

Ned *stares, sits, puts his head in his hands, pulls himself together.*

Ned   The point is . . . this is exactly what happened in *Vietnam* . . . a technological solution for a human problem . . . They tried every kind of technology they could think of to muscle people into line – B52s, Agent Orange, heroin, thought control, we throw everything we can at what is essentially a human problem – except humanity. As long as we have swarming technology and weaponised UAVs we'll never work with people, never negotiate, never make any effort to find a real solution to their misery, never consider cultural and religious antecedents, we're just going to bring out the big guns and move on to the next war.

Ross   But this isn't a big gun. This is a 'completely new paradigm'. A new paradigm for a new military morality.

Ned (*beat, stares*)   I don't buy that any more . . . I told you I changed my mind.

Ross   You changed your mind about that too?

Ned   Mm . . .

Ross   So you've change your mind about, what, 'everything'?

Brooks   As they say in the States: he 'flip-flopped'. I don't know how many suicide bombers you've met but I've met one or two. When I was stationed in Pakistan I was forever picking up suspects on the border, and what you don't understand is that a lot of them don't actually see their predicament as a 'human problem'. They're not interested in negotiating – they're not even that interested in martyrdom – some are secular. They just see it as a really good tactic in a war in which they're outgunned and overpowered – it's their own 'technological solution' – and it's purely a military requirement.

Ned   What I believe now is that if we attempt to negotiate without the leverage of weapons up our sleeve, it would be a more sincere form of negotiation than sticks and carrots and and and so . . . a more effective one.

Brooks   No. What if we can't negotiate because nobody will negotiate with us? The whole point about going to war is forcing people to the negotiating table.

Ned   This could be the thing that pushes us over the edge . . . never-ending war in the Middle East and we won't be able to negotiate our way out of it because nobody will believe in negotiation at all any more, they'll just want revenge, and we'll only invest in technological solutions because that's where the money is!

Brooks   This is our chance to *regain control*. I'm not going to get jingoistic here, or start crapping on about democracy – personally I think it's overrated. It only works in wealthy countries. In poor countries where there's nothing to lose it causes violence and chaos. Personally I think we need to be more *discriminating*.

Ross *nods.*

Brooks   But, you see, like it or not, we are in a situation here, from which we cannot extricate ourselves – it is hopeless – You and I now have a duty to do everything we can to ameliorate this. No – listen. Because every time a suicide bomber strikes, every time a young soldier or a humanitarian aid worker or journalist or some poor fucking welder from Wolverhampton is taken hostage and beheaded and we can't do anything about it because they're being shielded behind civilians . . . every time innocent villagers die because we dropped a five-hundred-pound bomb and it missed . . . just remember that this is a solution. Technological or otherwise, it's a solution. A *chance*. Something which offers *hope*. And so, you see, I think it's actually *wrong* not to try. Do you get what I'm trying to say?

Long silence.

Ned   I'm just an engineer. I work here like everybody else – listen – to the limit of my capabilities –

Brooks   You're frightened. That's OK. I'm frightened too sometimes. I'm frightened by my own brilliance . . . but I don't let it get in the way of things. Perhaps instead of having a big tantrum, you just need a holiday.

Ned   What do you mean?

Brooks   Nothing. I just mean it's been remarked upon by certain people. Some of your colleagues. That you've been getting a little 'tired and emotional' . . . You look like you need a holiday . . . get away from it all . . .

Ned   Who said this?

Brooks   Never mind who said it. It was said.

Ross   I think you need a rest, don't you?

Ned   Well, I do *now*.

Brooks   Have you ever had any counselling?

Ned   What do you mean – what sort of counselling?

Brooks   Just someone to help you think things through. Sometimes it's useful . . . sometimes if a person's worried about something, if they're stuck on a problem, if they're thinking along certain lines and they can't quite see the wood for the trees, it's good to just nudge them in the right direction . . . help them to see things a little bit more clearly . . . I could recommend someone . . . (*Pause.*) Or perhaps you could invest in a short course of –

Ned   What are you saying?

Brooks   Anger management.

Ned   What do you mean?

Brooks   Someone to help you understand the options . . .

Ned   What the fuck?

Brooks   You see, some of the things you've been saying, some of your more melodramatic notions, the paranoia . . .

Ross   You're not the easiest person to get on with, if you don't mind me saying.

Brooks   I agree. Absolutely. Don't you agree?

Ned   Why would I agree?!

Brooks   Just flagging it up.

Ned   Flagging up what?

Brooks   How people are thinking.

Ned   People think I need psychiatric help?

Brooks   Have you ever used antidepressants?

Ned   I . . . what do you mean?

Brooks   Just something to even things out a bit. Seroxat? Prozac? Nothing like that?

Pause.

Ned   No . . .

Brooks   Oh, that's funny, because for some reason we thought you had. (*Pause.*) What I heard was that a few years ago you were prescribed Seroxat by your GP . . .

Ned   W— who told you that?

They look at **Ross**.

Ross   It's usual to declare things like this in your funding application.

Brooks   Isn't that the one where people flip out and start, you know, murdering their wives and stuff?

Ned   Actually they tend to commit suicide.

Brooks   Not a bad idea.

Ned   What?

Brooks   I'm joking. Sorry. Carry on.

Ned (*beat*)   So now there's . . . is there . . . a file on me?

Brooks   What did you expect? Oh – the other thing is, you gotta stop telling people about this stuff.

Ned   Eh . . . ?

Brooks   You gotta stop telling people. It's Classified Technology. You can't talk to your family about it.

Ned *stares.*

Brooks   I mean, this is how you get yourself in trouble. You signed a thing. If you're going to go around mouthing off like this –

Ned   'Mouthing off'?

Brooks   I mean, with the greatest respect, and please don't take this the wrong way, but for the love of God . . . (*Laughs.*) What is wrong with you? Don't you know this stuff? Where did you train – *Disneyland*?

Ned   OK . . . listen . . . I didn't need them . . . I didn't even take the pills . . . I got better . . . I was misdiagnosed . . .

Brooks   With what?

Ned   It doesn't matter what. I didn't have it. So I didn't take it.

Brooks   Oh. And what did your doctor say about that?

Ned   He said I obviously didn't need them.

Brooks   Well, somebody obviously thought you did or he wouldn't have prescribed them.

Ned   No. My dad had . . . my dad died several years before in rather a dreadful way . . .

Brooks   What was dreadful about it?

Ned (*beat*)   What?

Brooks   What was so dreadful about it?

Ned   It was just an awful painful slow death. He couldn't eat . . . he got very frail . . . he was very frightened and angry all the time . . .

Ross   Oh no. What was wrong with him?

Ned   He had cancer. A rare form of cancer.

Ross   What was so rare about it?

Ned *stares.*

Ned   Look, I don't really want to go into it . . .

Brooks   Well, I'm asking you to.

Pause.

Ned   It was just . . . a terrible time. I'd just got married, I was spending a lot of time apart from my wife flying to the States. Flying all over the place for work. I missed her. I was apart from her for too long . . . I was under a lot of pressure to complete some critical trials . . . It was depressing. I was depressed. Understandably. In the end I chucked out the pills and bought a plane ticket home. I got better.

Brooks   You get very emotionally involved in your work, don't you? It's unusual. If you don't want to work, take voluntary redundancy, take a nice little retirement package, forget about California, forget about Britain for the time being, get a cab to Luton, fly with Easyjet to somewhere hot with your wife and don't come back for a bit.

Ned   Easyjet? Why Easyjet?

Brooks   We're not paying.

Ned *is on the verge of running out of the door.*

Ned   I'm going to go berserk in a minute.

Brooks   Sit down . . . I said sit down . . . I'm not done.

Ned *sits, blinking rapidly, increasingly nervous.*

Ned   You're a nutcase. You've escaped from somewhere . . .

Brooks   Be that as it may . . .

Ned   You're making it up as you go along.

Brooks   OK, calm down –

Ned   This is insane! It's insane!

Ross   Ned –

Brooks   Ned –

Ned   This is like a practical joke!

Ross   Ned –

Brooks   Ned –

Ross   Ned –

Brooks   Ned –

Ned   It's it's it's it's –

Ross   Listen to me –

Brooks   Relax –

Ross   Don't take it personally –

Ned   It's nuts!

Brooks   It's just how things work –

Ross   We're not blaming you –

Brooks   We're just urging you –

Ross   To make a decision – and hurry up about it – I know it isn't easy –

Brooks   Shit or get off the pot.

Silence.

Ned   What do you want me to do? What do we need to . . . ?
I just want to sort this out . . .

Ross   Is that what you really want? Is that what you're really
saying now?

Brooks   I think you're being very wise.

Ross   A rapprochement, as they say. Sounds pretty good to
me . . .

Brooks   Then we can all go home.

Ned *looks from one to the other, bemused.*

Ross *produces the contract, hands* **Ned** *a pen. He's reluctant to take it.*

Ross   You're more talented than you know. You can see
designs all around you – in birds, in bees, trees, the stars – you
can pluck a design from thin air and build it from nothing. You
can look at a machine, any machine and know how it works –
how to make it work better – how to stop it working. You're
an artist. That's why I'm being hard on you now. All they want
to hear from me is that you've changed your mind. You have
so many friends, a tremendous reputation, people hold you in
high regard and with such great affection. If you stop what
you're doing now, the world will be a poorer, duller, more
dangerous place. (*Pause.*) So what do you say?

Long silence. **Ned** *stares and blinks, extremely anxious.*

After a long pause he finally takes the pen.

Ned   Where do you want me to sign?

Blackout.

Two

Dan *is sitting anxiously where* **Ned** *was sitting.* **Ross** *is pacing about him angrily,* **Brooks** *is calmer.*

Dan   When was he last at work?

Ross   Six weeks ago. He came in to clear his desk . . . he was made redundant –

Dan   Well, he wasn't actually –

Brooks   Hold on.

Ross   He was offered voluntary redundancy with a generous –

Dan   That's not the case –

Ross   A generous severance –

Dan   Well, I don't think he really was –

Brooks   I'm not interested in that.

Ross   Yes, obviously it's a confidential matter –

Dan   Who else was offered redundancy?

Ross   There was a budget deficit – we needed to squeeze –

Brooks   OK, we'll get to this –

Dan   He was fired after he signed over the intellectual property. He did what he was asked to do, and you simply –

Ross   No, that's just not the case –

Dan   You sucked him dry –

Ross   Well, I disagree –

Brooks   All right –

Dan   And flushed him away like –

Ross   Not at all –

Dan   Sewage!

Brooks   I said all right –

Dan   He was treated like –

Ross   He stopped turning up for work.

Dan   Sewage! Do you think that's fair? Which part of that do you think is honourable?

Brooks   ENOUGH!

Ross   He stopped turning up for work!

Dan   He was in his studio!

Brooks   HEY HEY HEY HEY! I SAID ENOUGH!

Dan   Are you calling me a liar? Go to his studio. Go to his his his place in Earls Court –

Brooks   I've been to his place in Earls Court. I didn't find anything. Maybe I should go to your place.

Dan (*beat*)   It's got nothing to do with me . . .

Ross   Listen, I'm sure this is very upsetting for you, but –

Dan   I've got a practice to run! I have patients waiting for me!

Ross   I don't give a shit.

Brooks   All right, calm down. I know this is very stressful – it's stressful for all of us, but if we panic and lose our heads –

Ross (*ignoring him*)   Listen to me – your brother has now programmed a bug into the system –

Brooks   Did you hear me?

Ross   No, listen – into his own programme – which has rendered it useless. OK? He's sabotaged his own prototype . . .

Dan   Well, I don't believe that. I don't believe that at all.

Brooks   OK, I'm going to get to this in a minute –

Ross   He's built in a malfunction. OK?

Brooks   We'll do this in a minute –

Ross   He created an executional version and fucked up the GPS coordinates. There's an avionics malfunction and nobody knows where the seeker is looking. We wanted an indicator to show which weapon is selected and his indicator says 'no weapons selected' . . . And and and so even if we could launch the fucker it would target its own fucking launch pad! It's going to target its own launch pad. It's going to target its own base and destroy itself! It's a chunk of junk! We can't fix it and even if we could it'll cost millions! You're brother is a *child*! And and and your entire family is *mentally retarded*!

She wanders away a few steps, shaking her head, muttering to herself.

Dan *looks at her, then looks at* **Brooks***, bemused.*

Dan   There's no need to get personal.

Brooks   Did he take any money with him?

Dan   Not that I know of.

Ross   Seventy million he's cost us. Seventy million pounds at least –

Brooks   Be quiet, Angela. Have you got any details of his bank accounts?

Ross   He used a code to create an executional –

Brooks   We'll get to that.

Ross   – executional version and then he corrupted it.

Dan   Well, I don't believe there's a code, I don't believe there's a malfunction, I don't believe there was a redundancy.

Brooks   OK, just hold on.

Dan   I'm a reasonable man. I'm a pretty honest person. Not given to wild flights of fancy. And I don't believe a word of it –

Ross   He's a criminal. He is! There are laws against this kind of thing.

Brooks   I said – please – be quiet.

Ross   Look on his computer. Go through the hard drive.

Brooks We're going to look on his computer, it's all being taken care of.

Ross Find his codes. Go on, find his codes.

Brooks OK, we'll find his codes for you.

Ross Because – because this is a lot of money we're talking about.

Brooks (*standing up*)   OK. Great. Thank you. Thanks for your time. I've finished with you now. I'll take it from here.

Ross I am trying to help you.

Brooks Well, just for the time being you can help me by leaving. I'll get to you, later.

Ross Leaving? Here?

Brooks I'll get to you.

Ross I work here.

Brooks You will have an opportunity to say all this, later.

Ross *gives* **Dan** *a 'look' and goes.*

Dan What a fucking rude woman.

Silence.

Brooks Right, now we can get down to business.

Dan H— how do you mean?

Brooks 'Mano-a-mano . . . '

Dan (*nervous*) OK . . .

Brooks *studies* **Dan** *a moment.*

Brooks How you feeling?

Dan OK . . .

Brooks Holding up?

Dan Yeah, no, yeah . . .

Brooks   OK then. So where do you think he is?

Dan   I don't know where he is. I've said.

Brooks   D'you think he's in Italy? D'you think he's staying at your house in Italy?

Dan (*beat, vague*)   What house in Italy? I don't have a house in Italy.

Brooks   The house in Castellina that you bought with your wife. With Nancy. That's yours, isn't it?

Dan   Oh, *that* house . . .

Brooks   Have I got this right?

Dan   He's not there.

Brooks   Oh, isn't be? You're sure about that?

Dan   Let me think . . . (*Thinks.*) No, I'm pretty sure he's not . . . Last time I checked . . .

Brooks   Oh. So you checked?

Dan (*beat*)   Yeah . . . I checked . . .

Brooks   How did you check?

Dan (*beat*)   I rang the house . . .

Brooks   Perhaps he's not answering the phone . . .

Dan (*beat*)   I spoke to the gardener . . .

Brooks   And the gardener was in the house and he just picked up the phone?

Dan   Yeah . . . or . . . he could've quickly run in.

Brooks   What's this gardener's name?

Dan   Pedro.

Brooks   'Pedro' the gardener . . . Really? He's really called Pedro? Pedro's a Spanish name.

Dan   He is Spanish.

Brooks   So the house is in Italy but this guy is Spanish?

Dan (*beat*)   It's a long story. He he he sometimes cleans the pool too . . .

Brooks   You've got a pool?

Dan   Yeah, yes . . .

Brooks   Nice . . .

Dan   It's kind of essential in the summer months . . .

Brooks   Maybe your brother fell in the pool?

Dan *stares, worried.*

Pause.

Dan   I doubt it . . .

Brooks   No, he couldn't have, could he? Because he's not even there.

Dan   Yeah . . .

Brooks   So where do you think he is?

Dan   I don't know where he is.

Brooks   Yeah, but where do you imagine he is?

Dan   I've got no idea . . .

Brooks   Well, I've got no idea either . . .

Dan *goes quiet.* **Brooks** *stands and wanders around a bit.*

Brooks   Was he depressed when you last saw him?

Dan   He wasn't a million laughs, but he wasn't . . . What do you mean?

Brooks   Did he have a laptop? (*Pause.*) Your brother? A laptop.

Dan   Yeah, I think . . .

Brooks   Do you think he took his laptop with him?

Dan   I didn't see it anywhere.

Brooks   OK. Good.

Dan   Is that, is that significant, do you think?

Brooks   If he's using wireless we can track him.

Dan   Do you think he's just, you know, in the countryside somewhere, in the countryside with his laptop? Doing things on his laptop? In the countryside? In in in Wales or somewhere?

Brooks   Wales? Why do you say that?

Dan   He sometimes worked at an air force base in North Wales.

Brooks   What would he go there for?

Dan   I don't know . . .

Brooks   Then why did you say that? Why did you bring up Wales like that?

Dan   I can't remember.

They stare at each other a moment.

Brooks   What about his wife? Would she know?

Dan   He's separated from his wife.

Brooks   Maybe I could go and see her.

Dan   I don't really . . . Yeah, no . . . maybe . . .

Brooks   Maybe I could go and see yours.

Dan (*beat*)   I don't think that's wise.

Brooks   I'm not asking if it's 'wise' . . .

Dan   She doesn't know anything.

Brooks   What does she do?

Dan   Nothing. She doesn't do anything.

Brooks   Does she work?

Dan   She's a primary school teacher.

Brooks   Nice. How lovely.

Dan   Listen . . . it's a long way back to London and I've really got to try and −

Brooks   Take the M25, you'll be there in no time.

Dan   Sure, no, yeah, OK . . .

Brooks   It's a devil of a journey, isn't it?

Dan   Mm . . .

Pause.

Brooks   I think I'd go mad working here . . . all the noise . . . the constant drone of machinery . . . Can you hear that? Is it me or is it . . . ? Listen . . . a constant drone . . .

Brooks *cups a hand to his ear.* **Dan** *listens but doesn't really know what he's talking about.*

Dan   It's − yeah − it's . . . No, yeah . . .

Brooks   I'm pretty sensitive to noise . . . I'm like a cow in that respect . . . You know, I can hear things from miles away . . . especially machinery . . . I can hear machinery when it's not even on. Like, for example, I can hear a toaster when it's not even on . . . It's really getting me down actually . . .

Pause.

Dan   Couldn't you wear earplugs?

Brooks   I don't like sticking things in my ears. It's torture . . . I mean constantly hearing things is quite literally . . . This is how we torture people! (*Pause.*) Obviously we can't call it 'torture' . . . We call it 'psychological coercion' . . . But it is torture . . . Believe you me. (*Pause.*) Then there's what we call the 'silent approach', which is when you just basically go all quiet and look them in the eye until they go mental . . .

He looks **Dan** *in the eye.*

Brooks   Then there's the 'futility technique approach', which is when you sort of just play on all their doubts and fears until

they feel everything is hopeless and they can't go on . . . (*Pause.*)
The Americans tend to favour what they call the 'direct
approach', which is when you just basically just don't have any
approach at all, you just, you know, just really fucking abuse
them and stuff . . . But I don't have much truck with that . . .
Where's the accomplishment in that?

Silence except for the distant droning of machinery.

It's a fascinating business . . . don't you think?

Dan *stares at him as if he's mad.*

Dan   Are we . . . are we finished now?

Brooks   'Are we finished?' God . . . no . . . I wish! No, we
haven't even started yet, I reckon . . .

Dan   But I I I I I I I I I . . . I I I I I . . . I I I I just don't know
if I can help you any more than I have . . .

Brooks   Aren't you worried?

Dan (*panicking*)   Yes, I am, but I haven't done anything! I'm
a dentist! I don't know anything about this sort of thing . . .
I mean, you know, it's it's it's it's got nothing to do with me . . .
it's none of my business . . . !

Brooks   No, I meant worried about your brother.

Dan *stares.*

Pause.

Dan   OK, I'll tell you everything I know . . .

Blackout.

Act Three

One

Ned's flat in Earls Court.

Rain outside.

Various detritus, takeaway food containers, beer cans, bottle and newspapers littered around.

Ned *is in a chair, arms on the armrests, head back, mouth packed with cotton wool. He is extremely unkempt and unshaven, has no shoes, large holes in his socks, and pyjamas on underneath his clothes.*

Dan *is off in the kitchen.*

Dan (*off*)   Do you floss?

Pause.

Ned (*grunts*)   Uh.

Dan *returns with a glass of water. He's wearing latex gloves. He probes in* **Ned**'s *mouth with a probe and pocket torch.*

Dan   You should floss every day.

Ned   Uh-huh.

Dan   And brush your teeth after every meal.

Ned (*grunts*)   Mm.

Dan   You have an impacted wisdom tooth that'll have to come out. And you have a molar that's starting to decay but it's too awkward to fill. I should whip that out as well . . .

Ned (*grunts*)   Uh-huh.

Dan (*more probing, scraping*)   I can replace these fillings with white ones if you like. Cost you fifty quid a tooth.

Ned (*grunts*)   Uh . . .

Dan   You want these whitened? I'll give you the stuff, you can Do It Yourself. Takes three weeks.

*He finishes work, casually unpacks his probe, various bits of cotton wool and his fingers from **Ned**'s mouth and takes his latex gloves off.*

Ned *just stares into space.*

Dan *hands him a glass of water.*

Dan   Rinse your mouth . . .

Ned *stares at the glass of water, then stares at **Dan** oddly.*

Dan   Go on . . . give it a rinse . . .

Ned *rinses his mouth, swills, then carefully spits the water back into the glass.* **Dan** *watches, vaguely appalled.*

Dan   How much are you drinking? (*Pause.*) Ned?

Pause.

Ned   None of your business . . .

Dan   Well . . . you're ruining your gums.

Ned   I'm self-medicating . . . cures my anxiety . . .

Dan   Drinking doesn't cure anxiety, it creates it. It makes you paranoid and depressed and angry and confused – no, listen – and then it makes you fat and stupid and all your teeth drop out and eventually your nose goes red, and your liver collapses, you get cancer of the gullet, and you die in agony . . .

Ned   Which is when you really need a drink.

He drinks more water.

I hope you weren't followed . . .

Dan   What do you mean?

Ned   Followed, on the way here . . .

Dan   Followed by who?

Ned   Followed by, you know, somebody who's following you.

Dan   I don't know what you're . . . What are you talking about?

Ned   I think I'm under surveillance. It feels like I'm being followed. I mean, you know when you're being followed, and they know when you know when you're being followed, and when you follow somebody, you know when they know when they're being followed.

Dan   I see . . .

Ned   I think they tapped the phone. There's a sort of clicking noise on the phone. Every time I tried to phone you I got this strange clicking noise . . .

Dan   That's just my switchboard . . . It's just the receptionist, you know, putting you through.

Ned   Some of the motels I had when I worked in America were crawling with surveillance . . . They bug everything.

Dan   Maybe you need to be under surveillance.

Ned   What . . . ?

Dan   Sorry . . .

Ned (*stares*)   What do you mean?

Dan   It was just a joke.

Ned   Why did you say that?

Dan   No reason.

Ned   Why did you want to look at my teeth?

Dan   It was just a check-up.

Ned   You seemed pretty busy in there.

Dan   They needed a scour, they were filthy. I've got to say this, your oral hygiene is appalling . . .

Ned   Why were you trying to sell me all that treatment?

Dan   You need a lot of work done.

Ned   What are you up to?

Dan   It was just a check-up!

Ned   What did you put in there?

Dan   I didn't put anything in there!

Ned   You're going to give me implants. With with with a microprocessor . . .

Dan (*stares, appalled*)   Now what are you on about?! I don't know what you're talking about . . . ! I don't understand . . . !

Ned   A prosthesis with a-a-a tiny chip – a tracking device . . .

Dan   I don't even do implants! It's not my province!

Ned *goes into the kitchen, returns with a claw hammer and sticks the claw end in his mouth.*

Dan (*appalled*)   What are you doing *now*?

Ned   What did you do to my teeth?

Dan   I didn't do anything . . . !

Ned   I'll rip them out . . . I'll rip them out by the roots one by one . . .

Ned *latches onto a tooth with the hammer.*

Dan   Jesus Christ – don't – you'll wreck the enamel!

Dan *takes a step towards* **Ned**.

Ned   I'll break them off like sticks of chalk!

Dan   Put it down! I can't bear it!

Ned *takes the hammer out of his mouth and waves it at* **Dan** *threateningly, making him flinch and back up again.*

Ned   Why did you tell them where I was?

Dan   Don't vent spleen at me –

Ned   Why would you do that?

Dan   Don't blame me.

Ned   Well, I fucking do blame you.

Dan   I was dragged by my hair down to see your boss. I got a grilling from that prick Brooks. I took time off work to help you. Don't you think I've got my own problems? It's not all

Botox and holidays in Castellina. I go to work at seven in the morning, and stare into this rancid hole full of discoloured enamel until my eyeballs bleed, all day, every day, shrouded in the farty stink of other people's digestive tracts – until it's time to sterilise my gear and go home and help Nancy put the kids to bed. The kids never want to go to bed, that takes hours. Nancy never wants to fuck, that takes skill. Foreplay is like a game of poker. She never wants to go on holiday, and when we do go on holiday all she wants to do is come home again. I lie awake at night on my side staring at her rump wondering where the good times went, then it's time to get up again. I owe hundreds of thousands on my mortgage . . . and and and I'm doing this stupid training thing which will probably never even work because I've wasted all my time worrying about you!

Ned *takes the hammer from his mouth and chucks it on the floor. He smoothes his hair, fidgety.*

Ned   When I was staying at your place I just . . . I didn't read or swim or watch TV or anything like that, I just sat there . . . on a chair . . . outside . . . every night watching the fireflies. Fireflies are amazing . . . like little green light bulbs with wings . . . as if their entire head is on fire . . . and . . . and I spent a bit of time trying to work out how they actually work, fireflies, where the, where the actual fire, the light, comes from and but and I couldn't . . . I couldn't really work it out . . . I didn't have the vaguest idea . . . which is unusual for me. (*Pause.*) Then, after Brooks caught up with me, he took me to this fucking terrible sordid industrial dump of a place on the road to Poggibonsi and we stayed in this shitty sort of . . . apartment complex . . . No air conditioning, baking in the sun . . . cold at night . . . bleak . . . desolate . . . dessicated . . . wind-blown . . . lonely . . . confusing . . . wasps everywhere. He said we just needed to talk things over for a while. Before we came home. Debrief. There was no furniture . . . not a stick . . . I spent a lot of time just . . . standing around . . . nowhere to sleep . . . 'I need sleep!' I said. 'Let me sleep!' He didn't sleep either. Up at dawn . . . barging in and out . . . He made sure I was fed . . . made sure I wasn't too cold at night . . . very organised. (*Pause.*) I think my blood pressure must have been through the roof

because I felt very . . . strange. Very uncomfortable . . .
incredibly tense all the time . . . with this awful feeling of . . .
nausea and . . . dread . . . (*Pause.*) And . . . and so we talked
things over . . . he did most of the talking. Huh . . . he can
really talk. He can be very persuasive. In the end he said a lot
of interesting things actually . . . he he he really helped me get
things into perspective . . . helped me see the . . . the simple good
in what he was doing, I suppose, in a funny sort of way . . . I
mean, in a funny sort of way we're both . . . we're both right . . .
That's how I see it. He's just doing his job really. I quite like
him, actually. And I mean, once I'd given him the executional
codes . . . he was a pussycat.

Dan   Wait, what are you saying? What did he do to you?

Ned *stares at* **Dan**, *blinking.*

Ned   One of the things he said to me was: 'Everybody thinks
they're doing the right thing . . . nobody thinks they're doing
the wrong thing but just cynically carry on anyway . . . that's
what makes it hard.' (*Pause.*) The problem is . . . when you start
a project like this . . . you justify it expediently . . . you say,
'This is a machine, I have a responsibility as an engineer to
make it as effective as I can.' You you you you have to *shelve*
your personal morality, you cannot, cannot, must not let it
overwhelm your professional judgement. You have to discover
what is there to be discovered. And I discovered something.
And it filled me with . . . it filled me with joy. (*Pause.*) The
trouble with da Vinci is his flying machine was never made . . .
his war machines were never manufactured. He never had to
worry about a plane full of passengers dropping out of the
sky . . . He never had to worry about . . . consequences.

He blinks and stares.

Maybe you can help me . . . Is there a medication I can take?
Just to help me keep things in perspective and make me less
anxious?

Dan   A medication to make you less anxious about the
American Military-Industrial Complex?

Ned   Yeah . . .

Dan No.

Ned Oh . . .

Dan You should get some sleep, I need it too.

He tries to guide **Ned** *to the door but* **Ned** *stays still, rooted to the spot.*

Ned I don't sleep any more. Have you ever had one of those dreams where you've killed somebody?

Dan Not really . . .

Ned After I gave them the executional codes, I started having them every night. (*Pause.*) Silly, isn't it? People in defence don't have bad dreams about killing people. They have bad dreams about *not* killing people. (*Pause.*) Are you hungry? We should get some noodles . . . we never got those noodles . . .

Dan Listen, I'm sorry, I've been on my feet all day, I have to get back and put the kids to bed . . .

Ned Bedtime already? Have a beer with me, Dan . . .

Dan They'll want a story. Or two or three . . .

Ned I could come over and read them a story . . .

Dan No. Maybe on the weekend. When you've had a chance to, you know, have a shave and a bath . . .

Ned Why can't I come round?

Dan I just don't want you to. You'll frighten the kids.

Ned I want to see them . . . I've been looking forward to it for so long . . .

Dan I'm sorry, Ned . . . but they're not your kids, they're mine. Have your own kids.

Ned Fat chance of that.

Dan Why don't you go away for a few days? Stay in Castellina . . . Take Janie. I'm serious . . . you might patch things up a bit . . . have a swim, get some sun, drink some nice wine . . . eh?

Ned   Janie doesn't want to have kids with me . . . She said once that she could never raise children while I was working on a weapons programme.

Dan   Then she should be delighted with your progress.

Silence.

Ned   Have you spoken to Mum?

Dan   She said she was going to call you.

Ned   When?

Dan   When she gets a moment.

Ned   Why hasn't she called?

Dan   I expect she's just busy . . .

Ned   Busy? Doing what?

Ned *stares into space.*

Pause.

Dan   Why don't you come for Sunday lunch next week? Nancy's roasting a duck.

Ned   Lucky duck.

Dan   Will you come?

Ned   What's the point?

Dan   You'll see the kids. Have a shave and sort yourself out and come for a family lunch? Mum's coming. What do you think?

Pause.

Ned Yeah – no – yeah – no – I'd like that . . .

Dan   Just, you know, tread carefully with Nancy and don't say anything provocative. The kids want to see you. You know, they like you. They adore you . . .

Ned *is welling up, he pinches his nose with his fingers, hands trembling. He squeezes his eyes shut as he weeps silently.*

Dan *squeezes* **Ned**'s *shoulder.*

Dan   Don't worry . . . don't worry . . . you'll be all right . . .

Ned   Yeah – no – yeah – no – yeah – yeah . . .

Dan   We've all been so worried about you . . .

Ned *blows his nose, pulls himself together, disengages.*

Dan *gathers his coat, scarf, bag, umbrella and so on.*

Ned   I'll see you out. I'll walk to the tube with you . . . where are my shoes . . . ?

He looks around for his shoes, finds them, puts them on hurriedly.

It's stopped raining.

They listen.

Fancy a drink? There's a good pub by the tube, just opened . . .

Dan   I have to be up early, patients at nine . . .

He goes to the door.

Ned   We could go to the chippy. Where's my coat? Fish and chips. Mushy peas. Have a bath and go to bed. Nice early night. Up early, nice cup of tea . . . papers in the morning . . . get the job page . . . I'm not fussy . . . I could make toys, like da Vinci . . . (*Pulling on a tatty coat, buttoning it up.*) In the Uffizi in Florence there's a lion, a wooden automaton, made by Da Vinci for Francis I, which walks into a room by itself, comes to a halt before you, its head swivels, its chest opens and a bouquet of the most beautiful purple lilies emerges like a gift . . . a peace offering . . . I could do that . . . couldn't I . . . couldn't I, Dan?

They stand there in the half-light, looking at each other.

Blackout.

Methuen Drama Student Editions

Jean Anouilh *Antigone* • John Arden *Serjeant Musgrave's Dance* •
Alan Ayckbourn *Confusions* • Aphra Behn *The Rover* • Edward
Bond *Lear* • Bertolt Brecht *The Caucasian Chalk Circle* • *Life of
Galileo* • *Mother Courage and her Children* • *The Resistible Rise of
Arturo Ui* • *The Threepenny Opera* • Anton Chekhov *The Cherry
Orchard* • *The Seagull* • *Three Sisters* • *Uncle Vanya* • Caryl Churchill
Serious Money • *Top Girls* • Shelagh Delaney *A Taste
of Honey* • Euripides *Medea* • *Elektra* • Dario Fo *Accidental Death of
an Anarchist* • Michael Frayn *Copenhagen* • John Galsworthy
Strife • Nikolai Gogol *The Government Inspector* • Robert Holman
Across Oka • Henrik Ibsen *A Doll's House* • *Hedda Gabler* • Charlotte
Keatley *My Mother Said I Never Should* • Bernard Kops *Dreams of
Anne Frank* • Joe Orton *Loot* • Federico García Lorca *Blood
Wedding* • *The House of Bernarda Alba* • (bilingual edition) *Yerma*
(bilingual edition) • David Mamet *Glengarry Glen Ross* • *Oleanna* •
Patrick Marber *Closer* • Luigi Pirandello *Six Characters in Search of
an Author* Mark Ravenhill *Shopping and F***ing* • Willy Russell
Blood Brothers • Sophocles *Antigone* • Wole Soyinka *Death and the
King's Horseman* • August Strindberg *Miss Julie* • J. M. Synge *The
Playboy of the Western World* • Theatre Workshop *Oh What a Lovely
War* • Arnold Wesker *The Merchant* • Oscar Wilde *The Importance
of Being Earnest* • Tennessee Williams *A Streetcar Named Desire* • *The
Glass Menagerie* • Timberlake Wertenbaker *Our Country's Good*

Methuen Drama Modern Plays

include work by

Edward Albee
Jean Anouilh
John Arden
Margaretta D'Arcy
Peter Barnes
Sebastian Barry
Brendan Behan
Dermot Bolger
Edward Bond
Bertolt Brecht
Howard Brenton
Anthony Burgess
Simon Burke
Jim Cartwright
Caryl Churchill
Noël Coward
Lucinda Coxon
Sarah Daniels
Nick Darke
Nick Dear
Shelagh Delaney
David Edgar
David Eldridge
Dario Fo
Michael Frayn
John Godber
Paul Godfrey
David Greig
John Guare
Peter Handke
David Harrower
Jonathan Harvey
Iain Heggie
Declan Hughes
Terry Johnson
Sarah Kane
Charlotte Keatley
Barrie Keeffe
Howard Korder

Robert Lepage
Doug Lucie
Martin McDonagh
John McGrath
Terrence McNally
David Mamet
Patrick Marber
Arthur Miller
Mtwa, Ngema & Simon
Tom Murphy
Phyllis Nagy
Peter Nichols
Sean O'Brien
Joseph O'Connor
Joe Orton
Louise Page
Joe Penhall
Luigi Pirandello
Stephen Poliakoff
Franca Rame
Mark Ravenhill
Philip Ridley
Reginald Rose
Willy Russell
Jean-Paul Sartre
Sam Shepard
Wole Soyinka
Shelagh Stephenson
Peter Straughan
C. P. Taylor
Theatre de Complicite
Theatre Workshop
Sue Townsend
Judy Upton
Timberlake Wertenbaker
Roy Williams
Snoo Wilson
Victoria Wood

For a complete catalogue of Methuen Drama titles
write to:

Methuen Drama
A & C Black Publishers Limited
38 Soho Square
London W1D 3HB

or you can visit our website at:
www.acblack.com

9 780713 688054